W9-ASP-108

Fairmount   Sept 2020

This item no longer
belongs to Davenport
Public Library

FRIENDS
of the
Davenport Public Library

"Celebrate The Printed Word"
Endowment Fund
provided funds for the
purchase of this item

"Jasmine Holmes's *Mother to Son* is written for a far larger audience than just her own children; she has delivered a literary benediction to grace our bookshelves, challenge our earthly cultures, strengthen our feeble hearts, and point us toward lasting hope."

K. A. Ellis, Cannada Fellow and Director, the Center for the Study of the Bible and Ethnicity at Reformed Theological Seminary, Atlanta

"What a privilege to sit at the feet of Jasmine Holmes in these pages. In order to navigate her way through one of the thorniest conversations today—race in America—Holmes has relied on biblical wisdom to convey hard-yet-hopeful truths to her son. So much is yet to be done to repair the sins of the past; so much is still possible through the church of Jesus Christ, who carried our burdens and become the way of reconciliation."

Jen Pollock Michel, author of *Surprised by Paradox* and *Keeping Place*

"*Mother to Son* is more than a collection of heartfelt letters of a young mother to her new son. *Mother to Son* is a missive to America and to the church about what it looks like to hope, to fear, to long, to risk, and to love—all while instilling in ourselves and in those we love and are called to lead both a sense of belonging in the present and a call to invest in a future of greater flourishing for us all."

Karen Swallow Prior, author of *On Reading Well* and *Fierce Convictions: The Extraordinary Life of Hannah More—Poet, Reformer, Abolitionist*

"The love of black mothers for their sons defies easy categorization. It's at once fierce and tender. It's folksy and sophisticated. It careens toward indulgence but insists on growing up. Black mothers somehow combine both the romance all mothers feel for their sons with the realism required in a racially cruel world. The love of black mothers for their sons is a gift to the world—and the church. In these pages you will see why, as Jasmine Holmes speaks to her sons and to the church about her sons, about black boys, about black mothers, about hope and pain, love and fear, justice and gospel. Anyone looking for an honest yet hopeful exploration of what it means to be black, a mom, a wife, and a Christian—in all the ways those labels interact—will find a witty, womanly, biblical, theologically sound guide in Jasmine as she talks with her boys, and ours."

Thabiti Anyabwile, pastor of Anacostia River Church, Washington, DC

"As I read *Mother to Son*, I couldn't help but think of the many African American mothers who will read and be able to take a deep, long breath and say, 'I am not alone.' This book is rich in theological and foundational truth about God and about who we all are because of God. A treasure of a book."

Trillia Newbell, author of *Sacred Endurance* and *God's Very Good Idea*

DAVENPORT PUBLIC LIBRARY
321 MAIN STREET
DAVENPORT, IOWA 52801-1490

FOREWORD BY *Jackie Hill Perry*

JASMINE L. HOLMES

Mother to Son

LETTERS TO A BLACK BOY ON IDENTITY *and* HOPE

An imprint of InterVarsity Press
Downers Grove, Illinois

InterVarsity Press
P.O. Box 1400, Downers Grove, IL 60515-1426
ivpress.com
email@ivpress.com

©2020 by Jasmine Linette Holmes

All rights reserved. No part of this book may be reproduced in any form without written permission from InterVarsity Press.

InterVarsity Press® is the book-publishing division of InterVarsity Christian Fellowship/USA®, a movement of students and faculty active on campus at hundreds of universities, colleges, and schools of nursing in the United States of America, and a member movement of the International Fellowship of Evangelical Students. For information about local and regional activities, visit intervarsity.org.

Scripture quotations, unless otherwise noted, are from The Holy Bible, English Standard Version, copyright © 2001 by Crossway Bibles, a division of Good News Publishers. Used by permission. All rights reserved.

While any stories in this book are true, some names and identifying information may have been changed to protect the privacy of individuals.

Published in association with the literary agent Don Gates of The Gates Group, www.the-gates-group.com.

Cover design and image composite: David Fassett
Interior design: Cindy Kiple
Images: silhouettes of heads: © David Jackson
old paper texture: © Katsumi Murouchi / Moment Collection / Getty Images
hand-drawn patterns: © amovitania / iStock / Getty Images Plus
branch illustration: © CSA Images / Getty Images

ISBN 978-0-8308-3276-7 (print)
ISBN 978-0-8308-4819-5 (digital)

Printed in the United States of America ∞

InterVarsity Press is committed to ecological stewardship and to the conservation of natural resources in all our operations. This book was printed using sustainably sourced paper.

Library of Congress Cataloging-in-Publication Data

A catalog record for this book is available from the Library of Congress.

P 23 22 21 20 19 18 17 16 15 14 13 12 11 10 9 8 7 6 5 4 3 2
Y 39 38 37 36 35 34 33 32 31 30 29 28 27 26 25 24 23 22 21 20

For Phillip,

the hopeful black boy I married.

For Wynn and Langston,

the beautiful black sons he gave me.

You are my world.

Contents

Foreword

Jackie Hill Perry

Black boys have it hard in this country. I know not because I've experienced it myself but because I'm married to one who has. My husband, a black boy once, now a man with the same skin, has opened my eyes to that reality. Being with him is how I've seen that the burdens brown boys speak about carrying are not exaggerations. One time, we were going through TSA before boarding a flight for home. My husband's boarding pass was given a red stamp unlike mine. At security, my experience was ordinary. I went through the x-ray once. My husband went through as well, but upon handing his stamped boarding pass to the agent, he was told that he needed to be checked *again*. I asked one of the agents about the stamp and the additional security screening. "He was stamped because he looked suspicious," the agent said.

I wondered what made him *more* suspicious than I would be. Or anyone else for that matter. Was it that he didn't smile wide enough at the flight agent? Maybe it was because he made too much eye contact with her or maybe not enough? She might've thought him to be impersonal or maybe too personal for her liking. All of these were vain speculations though—a charitable practice in denial. We both knew that his skin alongside all that he was made him a potential threat to the safety of an entire airport. But even then, I knew it wasn't *just* the deep brown tint of his body, a tone that God providentially intended for him to have. It was that he was brown *and* boy. It is one thing to be an African American in this country; it is another to be that and male. There is something about the two being embodied in one that sets Americans on fire.

Jasmine's letters to her son, I think, are her way of turning her pen into a hydrant. Not only to put out the flames inside of individuals and communities. The heat coming from the unwillingness and perhaps inability to acknowledge that race and racism is a reality in our country. But her letters, a metaphor for water, are here to quench our thirst. To give us something that we all need: life. This life not springing out of nowhere but out of Someone. Jesus, that beautiful brown man that dignifies us all. Her words are anchored in a truth that isn't biased but rather a truth that sets people free—but they still must choose to pick up the glass and drink.

These letters are personal and yet applicable to us all. With child or without. Brown or white. Married or single. We may not all understand what it is to be her, a black mother with a brown boy, but we all understand what it is like to love. To care so deeply for someone that your affection becomes words, and these words a means to encourage, teach, remind, warn, and inspire. But I personally believe that Jasmine's words aren't just an expression of her love for Wynn, but the evidence of her love for you, the reader. If that weren't the case, she could've easily written each chapter by hand, bound them with string, and set them somewhere safe for Wynn to read when he is able. But instead, here they are, typed on a page, bound in a book, and in your hands to read right now. Her words to Wynn are just as much for you as they are for him. That's love.

Introduction

It was my friend Karen Ellis who first told me to "use my Wynnspiration."

Wynn is my son. As I write this, he's just turned two years old. No one could ever be more loved by his parents than my husband, Phillip, and I adore our little boy. He is extroverted, inquisitive, fiercely affectionate, and staunchly opinionated. He's discovering so much about this world and has yet to grow jaded by the ups and downs of finding his place therein.

I am five foot eight. My husband is six foot six. So we are expecting a little giant. And we know that from a very early age, he is likely to be the biggest kid, the strongest kid, and the one least likely to be seen by outsiders as a kid. We know that he may be perceived as more threatening and aggressive than his non-black peers. We know that, like his daddy and me, he might grow up with stories of having been made to feel *other* because of the color of his skin.

We want him to walk through life cognizant of these facts without becoming jaded by them. We want to teach him that he has incomparable value in the eyes of the Father in spite of the way he will often be perceived. Though this life will sometimes make him feel less than human, he is more than a conqueror through his Savior. Against all odds, we want to raise an optimist. Someone who knows that he might receive the worst that this world has to offer and still believes the best. Someone who cultivates glorious respites from the cruelty of the world by the grace of God.

We also want to raise someone who will change this world so that by and by the narrative that he has to tell *his* son—or maybe that his son will have to tell *his* son, or his son's son—will be different. We want to hold that tension of the *already* with the *not yet*. The already being that Walter Wynn Holmes is an image bearer, invested with identity, dignity, and significance, and that in God's economy his brown skin is nothing more than a glorious display of the creative purpose of the Father. And the not yet being the fact that sometimes the world does not see this identity, dignity, and significance, and that the results are often grievous.

A SERIES OF LETTERS

Karen's advice to use Wynn as inspiration fanned a flame that had already been growing in me. It was sparked by James Baldwin's *My Dungeon Shook*, his letter to his nephew about the racially charged climate surrounding the Civil Rights movement, and Chimamanda Ngozi Adichie's *A Feminist Manifesto in Fifteen Suggestions*, her letter to her best friend who had recently given birth to a daughter. *Between the World And Me* came later, but Ta-Nehisi Coates's observations to his son only fueled the growing fire.

I set out to write a series of letters to Wynn, not just about the racial climate of the country that he lives in, but about the conversation surrounding this racial climate. I want to remind him that his identity is firmly planted in the person and work of Christ Jesus and that because of that he has incredible significance to the King of the universe. I want to remind him of his dignity as an image bearer and to encourage him to respond out of that dignity, even to a topic as emotionally charged as racial reconciliation. Even when the topic concerns the brown skin that he lives in.

But more than that, I want these letters to be a testament of a mother's love for her son and of a sister's love for the body of Christ. Because when I speak about these topics, I want to hold my brothers and sisters in the Lord close to my heart, as I do my own son—my own flesh and blood. They are my blood-bought family in Christ, redeemed by the God who took on flesh to save them.

The twofold purpose of this book, then, is first and foremost to give you a glimpse into the heart of a black mother's love for her beautiful black son. There are conversations that I will have to have with my little boy—conversations similar to the ones my parents had with me—that are unique to our ethnicity. I will have to teach him, not just who God says he is, but how the world's view of him may sometimes differ from that of the most high God.

While the first purpose of this letter is an inward look at a mother's heart for her son, the second purpose is an outward look at a sister's heart for her siblings. As I raise my son in our current cultural climate, my desire is that we, as older believers, will work at daily changing that environment, making it a more welcome place for discussion, learning, and growth. That, above all, our goal would be to see brothers and sisters of every tribe, tongue, and nation dwelling in unity, not by flattening God-given ethnic and cultural identities, but by living in the gloriously diverse reality of those identities for his glory.

As we cultivate environments that celebrate that diversity, I want us to do so with patience, gentleness, and love. I want us to be quicker to hear than we are to speak. To believe the best of our brothers and sisters in Christ, even when we don't quite understand where they are coming from. To take the emotionally charged rhetoric of the world and supplant it with the unifying language of biblical truth. I want us to be slower to accuse and draw lines in the sand where the Word of God has done neither.

Cultural differences are beautiful, but they aren't ultimate. I see one side of this discussion clamoring to flatten the differences and the other crying out for their supremacy. Neither approach will do. Without the balancing influence of the gospel of Christ, we will become unable to empathize with other believers whose struggles and personal triumphs differ from our own. We will become unable to lay aside those differences when appropriate and embrace our sameness as blood-bought children of the most high God.

These letters are less about offering a systematic approach for how to think about difficult topics than extending what I hope is a refreshing vision for how to speak about them. I don't claim to have every single answer to the challenges we face, but I do know the hope that unifies us as we seek those answers. And that is the hope that I want these letters to proclaim.

I have hope for my son that he will learn to navigate this life with confidence, optimism, and joy. And I have hope for the body of Christ, that we will learn to approach these conversations with those very same traits. The tenderness that I feel for Wynn is the tenderness that I want us to display toward one another. It's the tenderness that I feel toward everyone who picks up these letters.

This is the gift that my "Wynnspiration" brought me, and I pray that it is a gift to the church. I pray that my sweet son is an even dearer gift to the body of Christ and that I can model the same heart that I hope is cultivated in him.

And I pray the same for you as you read these letters.

ONE

You Are Mine

Dear Son,

When I found out we were having a boy, I jumped up and down and clapped my hands with glee. Literally. You can see it on video. I shouted a triumphant, "I knew it!"

Both times.

Before I found out about your brother, people warned me that I might be disappointed about not having a girl, but the minute I saw him waving his little . . . sword . . . across that dark, murky screen, a genuine smile spread across my face warming me down to my toes.

Two little boys. All mine.

I have always wanted to be a boy mom. Blame it on the fact that your Uncle Trey was my best friend growing up and that I gained six brothers between my fourteenth and twenty-third birthdays. As a teacher, I have always loved the rowdy boys best of all. In fact, when I found out that I was carrying you, I was teaching a class of twenty-five seventh- and eighth-grade boys who alternately drove me crazy and gave me some of the most joy-filled days of my career.

I'm sure that if God ever blesses me with a daughter, she will light up my life in the same surprising way my sister did after five of my brothers arrived. And I'll be just as glad to welcome her.

But I'm glad you're a little boy all the same.

I want to begin these letters by telling you how I see you.

I know it's not as important as how God sees you, but as I look into your eyes I realize that I am the very first source of identity you will ever know. You're getting to an age now where we will start catechizing you—teaching you about who made the world, who made you, and why he put you here. But before it all, my heartbeat and voice were the first sounds you ever heard. You were fearfully and wonderfully made by a Creator who knows you more intimately than I ever could— but he made your frame to share mine for nine whole months.

So in these letters, as I explain where you fit into the world, I'm going to take the liberty of beginning with where you fit into your mother's heart.

You Are a Mother's Son

"In the beginning was the Word, and the Word was with God, and the Word was God. . . . And the Word became flesh and dwelt among us, and we have seen his glory, glory as of the only Son from the Father, full of grace and truth" (Jn 1:1, 14).

I found out I was pregnant again when you were just seventeen months old. Though we lost that little baby early—as we'd lost a little one before the Lord gave us you—I named him "John." During the five weeks I carried him, the book of John grew incredibly important to me.

The phrase "the Word became flesh and dwelt among us" was mind-boggling to me. Growing up in the church, I am familiar with the idea that God became a man, but until John, I hadn't ever really considered that God became a *baby*—a fragile little life wholly dependent upon his mother, Mary; or that Mary became a *mother*—a fragile human being wholly dependent on God to protect and nurture the baby inside of her.

The first chapter of John is powerful for many reasons. It establishes the Son of God as the Creator of the universe. It proclaims that Jesus is God. It heralds Christ as the light of the world.

I could go on.

But as I've carried each of my babies, for me the most mind-boggling part of the passage has become this phrase in verse fourteen: "And the Word became flesh and dwelt among us."

The architect of the universe designed my body to bring forth life and then he entered into that process by becoming a mother's son. The Creator of all things humbled himself by becoming a baby, wholly dependent on his mother for survival.

His flesh was sustained by the intricate processes that takes place in women around the globe. His mother was once a young girl whose body became a living sacrifice for him the same way that my body became a living sacrifice for you. Did she have morning sickness too? Did she put her hand to her stomach to feel him kicking and dancing? How in the world was she able to ride on a donkey while nine months pregnant?

Jesus had a mother. And she was once a pregnant woman. And she went through the pain of labor to bring the Creator of the world into his own creation. Mary and I have a lot more in common than

I sometimes stop to think: we are both women called to the incredible task of submitting our bodies to God's glorious purpose of bringing life into this world. Jesus became *flesh and blood*—a man, like you'll become—and it all started in his mother's body.

When Eve stood trembling before the Father as he proclaimed that her offspring would crush the head of the serpent (Gen 3:15), he was declaring, in part, that the pain that she would experience in childbirth would result in generations of women who would lead to Mary, the woman who bore Christ. The conqueror of the serpent would start his life here on earth as a babe in the arms of a mother. The conqueror of the serpent would begin his life here on earth vulnerable in the womb of a daughter of Eve.

Mothers and sons have been part of God's redemptive story since the beginning of time. My love for you is the echo of a heart that has been beating for millennia. And it's purposeful.

You Are a Mother's Redemptive Blessing

I will never forget that early Sunday morning when I padded into the bathroom and quietly opened the packet of a pregnancy test, trying not to wake your daddy up. We were the epitome of poor newlyweds, living in a five-hundred-square-foot apartment and barely making ends meet. Only a month had passed since our wedding, and we'd experienced what felt like more than our fair share of growing pains.

I still remember the way my hands shook when I saw the word *pregnant*. I don't know how long I sat there staring at it, willing it to sink in before I flushed the toilet, crawled back into bed, and looked at your daddy with wide eyes.

"You're pregnant," he said.

He ruins every surprise like that, by the way.

We were *so* excited about that little baby I was convinced was a boy. Our excitement lasted an entire month before the dating ultrasound revealed a baby measuring about a week too small—a little baby without the thrum of the heartbeat we had expected to hear.

My whole world fell apart.

I had never cried that hard in my life, although I've cried even harder since. My body went from feeling like the habitat for a glorious miracle to a sepulcher.

Your daddy and I sat in the car for several minutes afterwards, holding hands in stunned silence. I don't even remember what he finally said to try and comfort me, but I wasn't having it. I snatched my hand away and shouted, "He's *dead*. He *died*. I am carrying a dead, dead baby."

That sounds macabre, I know. But as a woman who firmly believes that life begins at conception, the fact that my child's heart had stopped beating sliced through me like a knife. I hadn't just lost the hope of motherhood. I already *was* a mother. I had lost my child.

Almost a year later, as I sat in the bathroom clutching a positive test on another Sunday morning, I felt a new twinge of fear. That fear would follow me through every prenatal appointment, but the one where we first heard your heartbeat is the one I will always remember most.

I sobbed as though my heart was breaking, but it wasn't. It was mending. And though you have a sweet life all your own completely separate from the first baby I lost, *you* were the first baby who showed me that my motherhood could be connected to joy instead of pain. You were the redemptive little rainbow after the storm of miscarriage.

I have two rainbow babies now and two babies I never got to meet. I don't pretend to love you more than a mother who has never experienced loss, but my love for you is different. And it's fierce.

You Are the Next Step in a Legacy

My phone number used to belong to your grandfather.

It's been my phone number for ten years now (and I'm refusing to give up that Texas area code), but every so often I'll get a call or text from someone looking for your pappy.

The parallels of that wrong number and my day-to-day life seem endless sometimes. I constantly have people asking me if they can speak with Pappy. It's the cost of having a popular preacher and writer for a dad. But while the scale might vary, any pastor's kid could probably say the same thing. Even as I'm knocking on thirty's door, some see my life as more hidden in Pappy than hidden in Christ.

You don't know it yet, but you've experienced this too. Right after we announced that we were having a son, more than one person asked, "Are you going to name him Voddie Jr.?" To them, it seemed like a completely innocent question, or even a joke. But to me, it felt incredibly disrespectful. I have a husband whose identity was completely bypassed in the name of celebrating celebrity.

On the one hand, I can understand that people are starstruck. I have a really good dad. In a landscape where fatherlessness is *the* political phrase buzzing around little black boys like you, I was not only raised in an intact home, but also by a dad who loves the Lord and has a passion for encouraging other families to seek earnestly after him. It's a gift that I could easily take for granted, but I try not to.

Thanks to my childhood as a homeschool student, he has been one of my favorite teachers, counselors, and confidants. We have a wealth of memories, inside jokes, and well-worn conversation topics. Growing up, he was my biggest advocate, my constant cheerleader, and my rock when the stresses of life overwhelmed me.

Pappy was an amazing earthly example of God's fatherly love toward his children (Ps 86:5). He protected me (2 Thess 3:3), provided for me (Lk 12:24), patiently instructed me (Ps 25:12), and led our family (Ps 5:8). He did all of these things imperfectly, of course—God is the only perfect Father—but he did them with love, commitment, and diligence. In so many ways, my father is the father I know that your daddy aspires to be for you, just as my mother is the type of mother that I'd love to be.

But my parents are still flawed human beings who aren't accountable for my walk with Christ. I'm responsible to God for my own obedience. I'm responsible for raising you, not just in the patterns my parents taught me, but in the pattern of Scripture. Their parenting was exemplary in so many ways, but I have an even more exemplary parent to follow in heaven.

And as you grow up in a Christian home with a fantastic grandfather and an even better daddy (says your biased mama), you are going to have to balance your beautiful legacy with your own personal responsibility.

You are the son of two parents who are striving to make a difference in the church. Your daddy is the hardest working man I know and one of the most well-connected men in our city—so much so that if I'm not recognized as "Voddie's daughter," I'm certainly known as "Phillip's wife." Your mama is planning on sending you to the school where she teaches, and you'll no doubt be "Jasmine's son" to more than a few there.

I don't want you to despise being known as one of us, but I do want you to know that you are created with individual worth and value before the Father. You were not made to bloom in our shadows.

In Psalms, Solomon tells us that children are like arrows in the hands of a mighty warrior (Ps 127:4). Arrows do a warrior no good if they stay in his quiver. They're made to be launched in battle.

Many people fail to consider that children aren't meant to remain in the shadows of their parents for the rest of their lives. They're made to be launched from their homes where they were trained to bring the good news of Christ Jesus to a hurting world.

All of the teaching and training my parents poured into me was for God's glory. I'm not ultimately a testament of Voddie's faithfulness, but of God's. And he intends not for you to be crafted into my image, but into the image of Christ (Rom 8:29).

YOU ARE THE OLDEST CHILD

You are my firstborn son.

Which means you're a bit of a guinea pig. I'm sorry. But if it makes you feel any better, I know how it feels. I was born in 1990, and my youngest sibling arrived in 2013. His parents are completely different from the bumbling just-turned-twenty-somethings who set out to raise me. They are wiser, more patient, more compassionate, and more directed parents to him than they were to me. Rather than resent him for that, I thank God for the evidence of growth in my parents' lives. If God had chosen, I could have come into the world in 2013 instead of 1990, but he decided in his glorious purposes that I would be raised by the youngins in all of their zeal.

God's purpose for you seems to be a similar track. You have the benefit of my energy as well as the handicap of my ignorance. These letters aren't the how-to of an experienced parent, but the hopes of a first-time mom. As I bungle through these parenting years, you might sometimes wish for a more experienced mama than the one I happen to be, but I'm so very grateful that you don't have her because she wouldn't be me.

This is the first time I've done this. And while I plan to do the very best I can, I know I will fall short sometimes, just like my parents. But I want to love you with the same fierceness with which I was loved and I want to do my very best to submit that love to the patterns I see in the Scriptures.

I hope you will look back on your young mama with grace. But I also hope that you'll look back on me and see a firm resolve to love you well. I hope you'll see some ways that loved you right. I hope you'll see a quickness to repent of the things that I got wrong.

These letters are not a picture of perfect parenthood. They are not the well-crystalized thoughts of a gray-haired, wizened woman. They are the real-time musings of a millennial mama who just tucked you in your highchair for breakfast and begged you for a kiss. They are the current thoughts of a late twenty-something woman who writes with her laptop propped just under a second-trimester baby bump. They aren't the oft-trodden pathways of the past, but a hopeful trailblazing into the future. They're not written for your eyes only, but for the church as well. Not as an expert, but as a layman showing all of her cards.

I ask you for grace in that. I ask them for grace in that. I trust God for grace in that.

You Are a Little Black Boy

Just this morning, I watched a video of two cops cuffing a young black man on the side of the road. He hadn't committed a crime. In fact, he was just sitting in the passenger seat of a car. He was riding with his (white) grandmother and her (white) friend, and the police stopped them because they thought he might be robbing those poor older women.

When they pulled the car over, told him to put his hands in the air, cuffed him, and put him in the back of their squad car, they saw a black man.

When I look at you, I see your brown skin. I see you in the face of the black teenager being cuffed for no reason. I see you when I teach my history class about the murder of Emmett Till. I see you when I hear people talk about black men in a way that questions their worth and humanity.

I see you everywhere.

But that is not the first thing I see when I look at you.

When I look at you, I see my son. I see the little jellybean whose heartbeat heralded more hope than I'd ever known in motherhood. I see the continuation of the family legacy that birthed me. I see the future of a biblical legacy that began before the dawn of time. I see my beautiful, bright-eyed, firstborn son.

I see a little boy full of joy. A tall-for-his age toddler who is friendly, exuberant, and loving. You never meet a stranger. You love to snuggle, blow goodbye kisses, and flirt with any beautiful woman you see. You love to hold my hand while we're riding in the car and lift up my shirt to kiss your baby brother in my belly. Sometimes, you even wave at my bellybutton, as though he can see you. You love any song with a beat and you're addicted to *Moana*. You don't like to nap without a bed full of stuffed animals and you refuse to go to sleep without first saying goodnight to everyone in the room—especially your mama.

Your brown skin is the same tone as mine, but wrought of a deeper hue like your daddy's. You are a replica of my baby picture with an obvious dose of Holmes thrown into your mannerisms and personality.

But because of your brown skin, you won't just be seen as tall for your age. To some, you'll look like an adult long before you're grown. Your exuberance will sometimes be mistaken for recklessness, your passion for anger. Your affection will make some people nervous, especially if your flirtation veers in the direction of the wrong white man's daughter. Your joyous dancing will indicate to some that you're wild, even threatening. Some people won't even take the time to get to know your tenderness.

Sweet boy, I do not say these things to jade you. As I teach you these lessons, I pray that they don't come from a place of bitterness or a life ruled by fear. I want them to flow from a place of wisdom. I can't just see you as my sweet little boy. I have to visualize the man that you'll become and I must prepare you to face the world in his skin.

But there is no better preparation for that than to know that you are not defined by the cruelty that some in this world wish to offer you. You aren't even completely defined by your mama's love. You are defined by the God of the universe who purposefully gave you that beautiful brown skin for his glory. No matter how the world might perceive you, hold your head high knowing that you are matchlessly loved by your Father in heaven.

And you will be fiercely protected by your mother on earth for as long as I possibly can.

Love,

Mama

TWO

You Are God's

Dear Son,

I just walked out of your bedroom like the creepy stalker mom I am.

Before your little brother started sleeping in your room, we never invested in a monitor for you. I'm a pretty low-maintenance type of mama, and even though you've been sleeping in your own room for quite some time, I never minded getting up in the dark and walking across the hall to nurse you. In fact, sometimes, I looked forward to it, waking up just before you and listening for your call.

You haven't been nursing for a while now, but I still sneak into your room by force of habit. I make my way over to peek in your crib and the sweet little nest you make with your blankets, stuffed animals, and the books I've slid through the bars to keep you occupied when you wake up a little bit too early.

Most of the time, you shift in your sleep when I come close, opening your eyes and whispering in that sweet toddler voice, "Hi,

Mama," before flipping back over and going to sleep. If I pick you up, you'll snuggle into my arms, and I'll breathe in your sweet baby scent, savoring the feeling of your soft hands around my shoulders and peppering your puckered lips with kisses because it's the only time you're actually still.

During those night vigils, I fervently pray for you—my baby who is no longer a baby. As I look down at your sweet, dimpled cheeks and the thumb that slips out of your mouth the moment you fall into a deep sleep, I think grand thoughts. I wonder who you will be when you grow up and I dream about watching it all unfold.

Being a mother is such an overwhelming phenomenon. I think about you all the time. Not always in the obsessive sneak-into-your-room-and-watch-you-sleep kind of way (sorry, kid), but because I feel the responsibility of being your primary caretaker and needing to make sure all of your needs are met. When you were a baby, I had to make sure that I fed you on time, packed enough diapers, carried a spare change of clothes, and wore the right kind of top to nurse you in. Now that you're a toddler, I have to make sure your diaper bag is packed, lay out your clothes for the day, and ask how you behaved at school to see if there's been a revival of your biting phase.

What is amazing to me is that, as much as I think of you, there is someone who thinks of you *even more* than I do. Since you'll be raised in the church, I know you already know the Sunday school answer to that one—it's Jesus.

While I agonized over having a healthy pregnancy, he already knew the sweet little boy you would become because he was in the business of forming you (Ps 139:13-16).

He's been in that business since the beginning.

You Are Made in His Image

The first three chapters of the Bible are as foundational as the first three chapters of any book. Although, they are more important because this book lays out the guiding purpose of our lives.

The well-trodden battlegrounds of our day—sanctity of life, gender, sexuality, race, stewardship, and authority—all begin at the very beginning of this book. Opening up Genesis, we learn that God is the author of humanity and that we are created in his image (Gen 1:27). He created us male and female with discernable differences (Gen 2:18) and charged us with the purpose of taking dominion over the earth he created (Gen 1:28).

And when he looked at Adam and Eve, he didn't just see the blond-haired, blue-eyed depictions often fantasized in Renaissance paintings, but two hosts for *all of the genetic material* needed to produce every tribe, tongue, nation, and people group that would populate the world. Adam and Eve held within them the promise of the nations —the promise of diversity. And it was good.

You Are Black on Purpose

It's no accident that you are black. You were made black on purpose.

God decided that you and your brother would be born as twenty-first century black boys to two black parents. He placed you in a lineage full of glorious complexity and gave you the task of learning how to glorify him in light of the ingredients he stirred into the pot of your identity. He invites you to delve into a deeper understanding of who you are as an individual so that you can see yourself in light of who you are in the grander story that he is writing.

You are black. And it is good.

I had an ultrasound the other day and brought home pictures of your little brother. When I handed them to you, you snatched them up, eagerly studying the face that looks so much like yours. With your brow furrowed and pudgy little hands gripping tightly, you said, "Hi, baby."

Your daddy and I were amazed watching your sweet little brother moving across the screen. We've seen my belly growing over the past eight months and we've known what's going on inside thanks to the constant updates from my many pregnancy apps. Still, there was something so special about seeing that little five-pound human pucker his lips and shield his face with his hands.

It reminded me of the day you were born. You came roaring into the world, and your daddy's was the first face you saw. He caught you up in his arms, looked down at you, and wept. "You were making a person," he marveled. "This entire time, there was a little person growing inside of you."

It truly is amazing. I was making a person. Or at least, I was the vessel for the person that God was making. He was crafting you each and every day, monitoring and guiding your explosion of cells, pouring into you the way he has poured into each and every person he's created since the dawn of time.

He was speaking, and it was becoming so. He was speaking, and it was good.

You are still a little sinner, miraculous origins notwithstanding. It's true that I'm much more liable to make excuses for your temper tantrums in a quest to fully understand the little person you're becoming than your daddy. "He's just tired," "It's a developmental phase," and "He doesn't understand" are my usual standbys whereas

Daddy cocks an eyebrow knowing you're just pushing boundaries. Still, I understand that you have a sin nature all your own, inherited from your first father, Adam.

Even though your sins often look a lot like those of your mother, Jasmine.

And that sin nature will crop up throughout your life. If you're anything like me (and you are), it will crouch at your door when it comes to conversations about race and identity.

You will be tempted to question the wisdom of God in speaking your brown skin into existence.

You will be tempted to disobey immediately when he calls you to hard tasks resulting from the color of your skin.

You will wrestle with shame in the face of a world that does not understand the beauty of your Creator's provision.

You will wrestle with pride in the face of a church that doesn't always thank God the way it should for your uniqueness.

Like me, you will wonder whether God is holding out on you for making you so different from the world you live in.

But I pray that you will come to an understanding of who you are that moves beyond your earthly heritage alone. I pray that your heavenly identity will not only supersede your earthly shell, but also give it deeper and fuller meaning as purposeful evidence of God's grace toward you and everyone around you.

My dear, sweet little boy, you were created in God's image. Your purpose is bound up in that one precious phrase: *imago Dei*. I pray that you will grow to acknowledge your Creator in all aspects of who you are, bowing your knee in gratitude for every single manifestation of his providence toward you.

I wish I could watch you safely sleep every single night for the rest of your life, but I know that the One who watches over you loves you even more than I do. I hope you know that too. Look at my love and measure his as ten thousand times more powerful. Then you'll have just barely scratched the surface.

He was so kind to make you mine for this tiny window of time. I pray that you are his for eternity.

Love,

Mama

THREE

You Are Beautiful

Dear Son,

The other night, your daddy and I were reminiscing about your birth. We do that a lot.

Your birth was one of the most beautiful days of my life, and though your brother's birth could not have been more different, it was equally precious to me.

With you, though, all I could do was marvel the first time I looked at you. Just moments before, you'd been in my womb, inhabiting my body, the only home you'd ever known. I had wondered what you would look like, what your voice would sound like, what it would be like to finally meet the little boy who wriggled under my hand when I placed it on my belly. And there you were.

While you didn't look particularly aesthetically pleasing at that particular moment (I'm sorry, little one, but you had a pretty pruny face for the first few hours), you were the most beautiful thing I had ever seen.

You still are.

You Are Seen With a Mother's Eyes

As I pen these words, I'm achingly aware of the fact that not everyone will see you with a mother's eyes.

Of course, I hear all the time how adorable you are. I get stopped in the post office while you're being your precious self. I pick you up from daycare and hear a day's worth of stories about your cuteness. I have to detox you after trips to Nana's because she gives in to your irresistible antics nonstop.

Once, while your daddy and I were enjoying a breakfast out with you, an elderly white man leaned over and asked, "How much do you want for him?"

The awkward pause that followed was burdened with a history of buying and selling, but your daddy handled it well by politely smiling and nodding at the bumbling older gentleman. "He's priceless."

Later on, when your cuteness inspired a family friend to ask the same question (it's a saying—we get it—but no), your daddy was able to explain the insensitivity surrounding such a joke given the fact that you could have really been for sale two hundred years ago. "Oh, yeah," our friend said. "Yeah. I can see why that isn't a good thing to say."

They can't have you, but I get why they "want" you no matter how awkwardly they express it.

Aesthetically, my love, you are undeniably pleasing. Those big brown eyes, those pursed little lips, the earnest set of your brow—I love your face. I know all mothers say these things about their children, but that won't stop me from joining the ranks of my fellow toddler-obsessed.

What I mean can best be captured in a story that you've heard me tell before. It's one that I remember hearing for the first time during

Black History Month as my brother and I perched on the edge of my parents' bed to watch the PBS miniseries, *Eyes On The Prize*.

I don't remember how old I was when I first saw the young boy from Chicago, grinning and dapper in the black and white picture that floated onto the screen. I don't even remember how I felt, exactly, the first time I heard about the white woman he allegedly whistled at, which led to his subsequent beating and murder. But I do remember growing up with that story year after year, first catching up to the boy in age, then surpassing him, then teaching young boys his age, and then carrying a son of my own.

I never wept at Emmett Till's story until you arrived.

I felt saddened by the event, but I saw Emmett in a completely different light as an adult. When I first taught his story as your mama last year, he was no longer simply a dapper, smiling young man to me. He was a little boy. A *beautiful*, bright-eyed little boy. The same kind of little boy that I shush at the end of a long class period or hold in my arms after nine months of pregnancy. The same kind of little boy as your brother.

Never did I suspect that I would end up living in Mississippi, not two hours from where that teenage Chicagoan was lynched. Never did his mother suspect when she sent him down for a summer in Mississippi that his death would be the flashpoint for a nationwide movement toward equality.

You Are Not Another Sob Story

Emmett Till was not beautiful to the men who lynched him. He was not a child. He was not full of potential. He was an object of hatred, and that hatred sparked murderous consequences.

I see a child on summer vacation.

They saw an animal in need of a lesson.

I see a handsome young man with the sweetest smile.

They saw a threat to their way of life.

I see a young boy who escaped the Jim Crow South during the Great Migration, destined for greater things.

They saw an upstart who needed to be put in his place.

More than three thousand black people were lynched in America following the Civil War. We'll talk about other aspects of your history in letters to come, but know that this number is not inconsequential. Some will compare it to acts of genocide that occurred in numbers climbing toward the *millions* and they will tell you that your statistics couldn't possibly compare.

My love, do not fall into this trap. Do not dehumanize the victims of other murderous acts by joining a game of *whataboutism*. If someone brings up the millions of Jewish image bearers who were slaughtered during the Holocaust, weep with them. If they harp on the genocide of abortion's body count, agree with them.

But know that you are discussing two different heinous acts.

When I was eleven years old, I watched as a plane flew into the World Trade Center. I didn't know it then, but this calculated attack would change the course of American history. Air travel, immigration activism, and American warfare would never be the same. Our peace was stolen for an entire generation.

If you had asked eleven-year-old me to calculate just how many people had been slain in those attacks, given how they would come to impact our country, I would have guessed *millions*.

But the number was actually in the thousands.

Nearly the same as the number of black people lynched during the Jim Crow era.

Jim Crow wasn't black genocide. The ultimate goal in the lynching of Emmett Till was not to snuff out an entire generation of little black boys.

No.

The ultimate goal was to forever alter the perception of the other black boys left behind. Like a terrorist attacking the heart of American ideals of safety and security, lynch mobs used fear and the threat of violence to keep black boys in check. They existed to embed a vein of fear and inferiority in the complex identity of black youths in America.

And for so many years, in so many ways, it worked.

You Hold a Mother's Fear

My fear for you, my son, is not so much that you will be lynched like Emmett Till.

Make no mistake, I will train you—as I was trained—to respond to authority in a way that will make you appear as nonthreatening and compliant as humanly possible. And I will hope and pray that this compliance will serve as some kind of barrier against the brutality that your young black form may incur. I will watch every news story of a black man gunned down by police with a twinge of fear, wanting so badly to trust that those charged with protecting our communities would not harm you without just cause, but fearing every scenario where they might.

But the possibility of violence against your body is just a small part of the fear your mother holds for you. My son, what I fear most is the way that the politicizing of that violence, and of the black bodies it sometimes harms, will impact your *mind*. Will you become desensitized by the death of black men, shrugging off injustice because it makes you uncomfortable? Will you become paralyzed by the death of black men, locked in an endless downward spiral of fear and grief? I truly hope not.

I began wrestling with these questions early in your life.

A few days after you were born, Philando Castile, a black man, was shot by police officers in the neighborhood where I'd spent the previous nine months carrying you. Before his body was cold, people across the country joined a chorus of lambasting the violence and unworthiness of the black community and vilifying the man who had just been killed. Then, about an hour later, someone sent me a tweet calling your grandfather a coon for his response to a past police shooting and sarcastically hoping that my husband wouldn't be unjustly gunned down.

I sat in a hotel room, four weeks postpartum, nursing you and watching as tweet after tweet poured in to analyze the situation, treating Philando not like a slain man, but like a pawn in political maneuvering.

As I reflect on Philando's death and think about the man you will become, I feel a burgeoning burden to teach you how to walk the taught tightrope between knowing the media's tendency to manipulate you with political statements and grieving the slaying of an image bearer.

As people clamor for more details, respect the fallen. Take a moment to mourn the fact that lungs the Lord filled with air have breathed their last breath. Remember that this human being was someone's son, brother, father, lover. Take a beat to pray for those whose lives will never be the same.

My son, your body is worth so much more than a hashtag or a political soundbite. And hear me: so was Philando's. And so are the many others you may be tempted to distance yourself from in the days to come.

You Really Are Beautiful

You are beautiful, not because "black is beautiful" is an in idea right now, but because you are fearfully and wonderfully made. And I tell you this not to pat myself on the back, but to model a message that we should all be proclaiming: the purpose of your ethnicity transcends this tiny political moment. You are not *more* beautiful because you are black, but part of your unique beauty comes from the rich heritage that the Lord has woven into your melanin.

He made you a little black boy on purpose. He stuck you into this particular moment in history with intention. I am not your mama on accident.

You Are More Than a Black Boy

A couple of years ago, a well-known white apologist recounted the story of a young black boy who treated him disrespectfully for no apparent reason. After mentioning how the boy rode away flipping him off, the man mused that the poor black kid probably came from a fatherless home and, frankly, didn't know any better.

The firestorm that ensued confused the apologist and many of his followers. We've all read the statistic that 70 percent of black kids grow up in fatherless homes. What was wrong with him pointing it out?

What they didn't understand was that distilling this boy's rude act to a calculation dehumanized a knuckleheaded teenager who could have just been having an off day. As a teacher to many teenage boys (and sister to more than one), I can tell you that those without a father have not cornered the market on needing to think before they act. And as the wife of a man who grew up without a father in the home and the daughter of another, I can assure you that their mothers worked hard at teaching them how to show deference to their elders.

But because this boy was black, he was lumped into a well-worn stereotype that sees black people not as individuals, but as a calculable monolith. And, ironically, some of the same people who would argue that race is just a social construct began using the statistics of that construct to back up their assumptions about yet another black body.

When Emmett Till was falsely accused of the crime that cost him his life, he was seen as nothing more than a black boy and, therefore, a threat.

Emmett's brown skin was beautiful, but it did not make up all of who he was.

And neither does yours.

As you grow into the young man God has purposed you to be, I am so excited to see all of your unique aspects fitting together for his glory. Your dad wants you to be a world-class athlete. I want you to be a Pulitzer Prize–winning author. But whatever you end up doing, you will be remarkable, because we serve a good and creative God.

In the heat of conversations about the worth of black bodies, I want you to remember that you are *more* than a black body. You are more than the threat that some people will immediately perceive you as. You are more than the victim or martyr others are so eager to take you for.

You are fearfully and wonderfully made. And you're precious. Not because you're one of the boys with a father at home or because your mother would *snatch a knot in you* (to borrow a much-used phrase in many a black household—no literal knots will be snatched) if you flipped off an older white stranger on a bicycle. You are precious because God breathed life into you in his divine timing and for his divine purposes.

He created you in his image.

And you're beautiful.

Love,

Mama

INTERLUDE

I Didn't Know I Was Beautiful

Dear Son,

When it comes to skin color, you will soon learn that black folks have a tendency to see it in shades.

And the message my mother got from her grandmother growing up was that the lighter the grandchild, the more beautiful.

I've shared the story of your great-grandmother before.

Your great-great-grandmother was a mulatto woman. She spent her youth passing as a white lady and married the fairest black man she could find. When she became a grandmother, she would always give her lighter grandchildren (of which Gram was one) a Kennedy half dollar coin when she came to see them, and she would give her darker grandchildren a quarter.

This blatant display of favoritism carried down into our generation with an older relative who exclaims every time she sees me, "Have you gotten . . . darker?" Gram, who married Pappy—and will call him a "giant of a chocolate man" to make you gag someday—taught me to say, "I sure hope so. I'd love to be chocolate."

My mother's great-grandfather on one side was full-blooded Cherokee, and the one on the other was full-blooded Choctaw. We've already talked about her great-grandmother, who was the daughter of a white plantation owner. We have diversity by the bucketfuls and a blue-eyed grandfather to prove it. But while my mother and her sisters grew up with the not-so-subtle message that brighter skin is better, I grew up with parents who showed me the beauty of all sorts of shades.

I remember the first time I watched the documentary *Dark Girls*, which highlights the fact that the favoritism of light skin is still rampant in our culture.

And it's not just among black women.

We all want to be bronze beauties of ambiguous origins.

I remember reading a magazine survey in my early twenties about how in the eighties, blonde and buxom was the national goal, while in the new millennium, we'd all give our left arms to look like the racially ambiguous chick.

Growing up, I can't say that I ever wanted to be lighter skinned than what I am. My mother wouldn't hear of that. But I was surrounded by people who claimed to be colorblind, which kept me from knowing that being black was beautiful. I got weird comments about my lips, my nose, my hair—even when they weren't cruel, they made me feel "other" and not pretty.

I thought it was, at best, a bit awkward—something that made my peers uncomfortable and needed to be downplayed so as not to take the focus off of the gospel. In trying not to draw attention to my skin tone, I became ashamed of it for a season.

I don't know when the switch turned on in my brain, but I think having so many beautiful younger siblings of varying shades and being part of a family that celebrated those shades helped me. From your Uncle Judah's fair, Kennedy-half worthy skin to your Uncle Micah's enviable chocolate hue, I fell in love with the beauty in my younger siblings and started to see the beauty in myself.

I remember my very first time reading *Roll of Thunder*. Mildred D. Taylor described Papa's skin as the color of pecans, and I never forgot it. She showed me that there was beauty within the variance of a skin tone that was so often looked at as monolithic other.

My skin was created for God's glory. And while I could draw myriad Punnett squares and talk Mendelian genetics with you all day, it is only the uniting beauty of the gospel that gives us a handle on just how lovely diversity really is.

I serve a God who has called "a great multitude that no one could number, from every nation, from all tribes and peoples and languages" (Rev 7:9) to partake as sons and heirs in his kingdom (Gal 4:7). I serve a God whose love for us transcends lines of gender, class, and ethnicity and who allows our horizontal love to do the same (Gal 3:28). I serve a God who put chestnuts, chocolate, caramel, butterscotch, and pecans all under the same roof just because he's creative like that.

I serve a God who sees chestnuts when he looks at my skin, and who put them there to be unabashedly beautiful for his glory.

The answer to favoritism between light and dark skin isn't to stick our heads in the sand and claim we don't see color, because that is to ignore the beauty that the Lord poured into our skin.

It's also disingenuous, because everyone sees color. My white friends see the difference in their hues, from alabaster and olive tones to enviable bronze tans. They talk about their "brassy" blonde hair and platinum hues, their sea-blue or blue-green eyes, because they note the differences.

And it's okay to note mine too.

So, son, I want you to hear me when I say this: you are part of a gorgeous tapestry the Lord is weaving in his creation. Whatever your shade, hair color, eye color, or stature, the Lord gave it to you on purpose and for his glory. I love your chocolate skin.

I may or may not have started praying for it the minute I fell in love with your mahogany-hued daddy.

And I'm not one ounce ashamed of it.

Love,

Mama

FOUR

You Are American

Dear Son,

You are currently obsessed with *The Snowy Day*.

Every day when you wake up, you walk into the living room and use your sweet, nasally little voice to ask for "Snow." You sit and intently watch almost the entire special, which is pretty impressive given your short attention span. Your face lights up as Peter walks across the screen, his brown skin an echo of your own.

I have a picture of you as an infant sitting in my lap, transfixed by Peter's snowy antics as captured in the work of Ezra Jack Keats, a Jewish author who decided that little black children deserved to have a little black hero in their books. You and I love Keats so much that your daddy and I named your baby brother Ezra Langston after your favorite author and mine. As much as I longed for your favorite piece of literature to be *Where The Wild Things Are* like it was for me, the fact that you choose Peter over Max and *Akili and Me* over *Caillou* (thank the Lord) illustrates a truth that I have always known: representation matters.

When it comes to the fractured political landscape of your country at this writing (and, really, at any writing since its founding), I imagine that there will be those who read that phrase and roll their eyes. Representation does *not* matter, they'll say. You should be able to love Stan Lee's Peter Parker as much as you love Ezra Jack Keats's little Peter, and it shouldn't make a lick of difference to you how melanin-packed their skin is.

But you are not a political pundit yet. You're only two years old. I didn't tell you to love Keats. I didn't tell you to be mesmerized by *Little Bill.* But you are. And even though I grew up loving Spider-Man so much that he made an appearance in fondant on my wedding cake, I remember feeling the same way about Suzie on *Rugrats.* There was something special about seeing a little brown-skinned girl. There was something special about seeing part of *me.*

It's the same reason why, when I was eighteen years old, the Obama campaign struck a chord in me. Despite myriad political differences, I found myself transfixed by the would-be first family.

I will never forget that day, standing in line at the polls with my mom, hands sweaty, eyes bright, heart pounding. I had never been so excited about anything in my entire life. When I got up to the desk and said my name, the poll worker hesitated.

"I don't see you anywhere on my list," she said, her voice wandering a bit.

I felt a lump forming in my throat, tears stinging my eyes. I couldn't *not* vote. Not today of all days. Your gram sensed the emotions coming over me and placed her perpetually soft hands on my shoulders. "Could you check again?" she asked.

And sure enough, there was my name.

As I stepped into the voting booth, the tears I'd kept at bay flowed anyway. At eighteen, I was still chock-full of so much idealism about how that vote could hold sway over the future of my country. I was overwhelmed at the sacrifices it had taken to make this moment possible, from suffragette marches to battered black bodies hanging high in the Jim Crow South.

When I got home, I wrote an article on my blog about everything that moment meant to me and spent a great deal of time expressing how meaningful the election of the first black president was to a young black American woman.

That night, at a church event, I had several people walk up to me and express concern over my piece:

"You know he's a flaming liberal, right?"

"He's really only half black."

"He's a Muslim. He probably wasn't even born here."

I hadn't voted for President Obama. I had voted for Ron Paul and had been pretty vocal about my young spitfire Libertarian ways. But the fact that I even had the nerve to express positive emotion over the election of someone with whom they were so ideologically opposed rattled some of the people in my community.

For them, the complex network of emotions that I had experienced standing in that voting booth was incredibly simple: he is a Democrat. We are Republicans. We do not fraternize across party lines.

You Are a Representation That Matters

The same people who barked at me for my wide-eyed enthusiasm about a black president and who assured that representation *absolutely did not matter* were not above using representation when it suited their own political ends.

For instance, you will often hear someone say, "Race is just a social construct" in response to issues of identity and ethnicity. But that same person will go on to cite statistics about how black fatherlessness breeds black criminality. Race does not matter to this person until it can be used to lambast the black community for its shortcomings.

Or maybe you'll hear someone say, "We need to stop getting so caught up in the color of people's skin. We ought to be colorblind." But if you watch them long enough, they'll use a black religious or political figure (sometimes your own grandfather) to try and trump others in an argument. Race doesn't matter until Thomas Sowell just happens to be a black voice who agrees with them and is, therefore, doubly influential.

You might even hear someone say, "We need to get beyond all of this talk about *coonery* and *house slaves* when it comes to political discourse. Black conservatives don't deserve to be called these rude names." But then the same person will go on to talk about the democratic plantation, planting black Democrats as mindless drones who sacrifice their morals to stick closely to party lines (as if they are the only ethnicity who does such a thing, and affiliation with the Democratic Party is the only way to do it).

You see, race *is* a social construct. And it also matters. Not in the sense that it changes the core of who you are—that is hidden in your identity as an image bearer of the most high God—but it will always matter in these kinds of political conversations.

If you don't believe me, pull up any black conservative pundit who is gaining traction in the social media world. I guarantee you will find at least one speech of them waxing eloquent about how they have forsaken their kinsmen to take a more reasonable path to conservatism. It reminds me a bit of a Pharisee loudly praying, "Praise God that I am not like other men!" and patting himself on the back for being victimized by the liberal wolves who are (more than likely) now shunning him.

As a black man, whatever your party affiliation, your skin color will garner enemies. From the Left, they will wonder why you've chosen a path so different from other people who look like you. Many from the Right will lump you in with the other "socialist drones." As a black man, people will jockey for your voice, your platform. Because both sides understand that representation *does* matter. The Left wants you because there is strength in their number of brown voices. The Right wants you because the comparative lack of black volume will make you even more dynamic.

And our country is so polarized that you'll just get lost in the middle if you're not careful.

You Are Complicated

So where should you fall?

The answer is complex.

I know that even that sentence is an affront to many evangelicals, because abortion statistics will be *the* single-issue voting factor that drives them to republicanism.

Abortion is heinous, my son. Not only that, but it inordinately affects black bodies and black communities. The day you were born, about nine hundred other black babies were slaughtered. Black Americans only make up 13 percent of our population, but account for over 30 percent of our nation's abortions.

This is genocide.

While Margaret Sanger's racism has been largely exaggerated in comparison to the rest of her American contemporaries (the woman was a classist as much as a racist, and if Abe Lincoln gets a pass on his ideas toward black Americans because he was "a man of his time," then I don't think Margaret deserves the title of antichrist all on her own), Planned Parenthood makes bank off of the murder of black babies in the womb.

Because of this, every single issue of race and ethnicity in the political sphere often bounces right back to abortion. It is impossible to have a conversation about racial disparity or systemic injustice without hearing about the war on black babies in the womb.

I don't want you to roll your eyes at this. You have uncles whose mothers sat in abortion clinics and very seriously considered ending the lives of their children before they chose to place them in our family. This issue is near and dear to your mama's heart, and I want it to be near and dear to your own. But I also don't want you to diminish the issue to a cheap political shot.

Here's what I mean: black abortion does not happen in a vacuum.

Unless you truly believe that black mothers are more bloodthirsty, ignorant, or depraved than their white or Hispanic counterparts, there has to be something else going on behind these numbers. And while the Republican Party's bread and butter is paying no attention to the Man behind the curtain, the Democratic Party's usual stance is to pretend that there is no curtain and focus solely on the Man.

Abortion rates aren't the only statistics that differ in the black community. At this writing, I am pregnant with your little brother. And though our family has escaped the poverty rates, incarceration rates, and unemployment rates that have plagued the black community for generations, statistics show that, no matter how well educated I am, I have a higher chance of dying in childbirth than any other ethnicity of woman in the United States. And your brother is more likely to be born premature or to die as an infant than any other ethnicity of baby.

Growing up, my conservative friends never stopped to ask why these realities were epidemic in the black community. They just seemed to instinctively take for granted that they *were* epidemic. And while they wanted to save black babies from being aborted, I heard very little conversation about how to save black communities from the blights that attacked children once they were born.

Don't mishear me: systemic injustice is not an excuse to take the life of an unborn child. Period. But the reasoning behind the decision to do so might take us a little bit deeper than picket lines and homemade signs.

And that's scary, complex stuff.

But complexity is only okay sometimes.

You see, my Obama-bashing friends were not strangers to the complexity that I was trying to express.

Or at least, they should not have been.

They themselves boasted a variety of complicated heroes, both political and religious. They prized Abraham Lincoln or Stonewall Jackson, Jonathan Edwards and George Whitefield, Thomas Jefferson and George Washington.

Now, son, by the time you read these words, I hope I will have taught you both what is exemplary about these men and what is heinous.

I hope you have learned how God used Abraham Lincoln to end slavery, even though he claimed that he never wished to do so, and that Stonewall Jackson fought valiantly for many state rights that I would uphold, but also for a state's right to slavery. I hope you've learned that Jonathan Edwards could preach a *lion* of a sermon, but that he also participated in man-stealing by purchasing slaves, and that George Whitefield helped spark a massive revival in America, but made Georgia a slave state. I want you to marvel at the ideological tenacity of Thomas Jefferson and also realize how diametrically opposed he was to matters of faith. And I want you to know about Sally Hemmings. I want you to see George Washington as a man of quiet conviction—so quiet that he waited until *after* he died to free his slaves.

We love to picture our heroes as spotless and without sin, but son of mine, you know that the only hero who fits that description is Christ Jesus. And while, like me, you may grow up surrounded by people who want to make excuses for these shortcomings so that they can continue to prize their most cherished heroes, I want you to stand apart from such a simplistic understanding of human nature.

It's because of this simplistic understanding of human nature that we have a tendency to excuse the inexcusable.

"Whoever steals a man and sells him, and anyone found in possession of him, shall be put to death" (Ex 21:16).

In spite of the fact that some slave owners may have, indeed, been God-fearing men, our nation's laws provided absolutely no inducement for them to practice their faith, leaving some of the most vulnerable members of society completely unprotected. Even if we forget how African slaves arrived on American shores—packed like sardines on a perilous passage, ravaged by every malady from rape to disease—the testimony of the way that the American judicial system dealt with those slaves once here screams of an inequity found nowhere in God's Word.

"But who sold them?" your friends will someday reply.

And I hope you won't waver when you answer that. Yes, Africans sold their brothers and sisters into slavery in such large numbers that the economy of large swaths of the continent was adversely affected when the slave trade ended.

But I hope you will also realize that this question is a deflection because our American heritage is the conversation at hand. And that heritage often claims to be a Christian one. While some Christian missionaries were making inroads to bring the gospel to the unreached peoples of Africa, so many more self-proclaimed Christians were participating in this sinful enterprise. The penalty for man-stealing and child-murder is the exact same in the Old Testament, but our patience for those in the former category as "a product of their times" differs radically from our blanket condemnation of those who endorse the latter in spite of the modern air they breathe. Why is that?

I know how awkward it is to be the only black kid in the classroom when the conversation shifts to slavery. I used to feel so uncomfortable, shifting in my chair and avoiding eye contact with my staring classmates. "I am more than this," I wanted to tell them.

You are more. I am not trying to make slavery the basis for your identity, which is why I have spent so much time talking about those other aspects. But I would be remiss if I did not begin this conversation about your Americanness with the way that our ancestors got here, beloved.

I would be remiss if I did not teach you that American chattel slavery was not just a blind spot. Blind spots that lead to the dehumanization of people made in the image of God aren't just blind spots. They're sin.

And America's *sinful* legacy of chattel slavery should not be glossed over by stating that "everyone else was doing it" any more than I want you to sit silently by while children are aborted because "everyone else thinks it's okay." The social and economic issues that contributed to the extension of American slavery for years were complicated, as is the background of the abortion debate, but they deserve no less indictment.

None of these things is beyond the blood of Christ. I feel the need to pause and say this because sometimes it gets forgotten. The only answer for the blight of racism on our nation's history and in the shaping of our identity is the blood of Christ. Apart from him, we have no basis for true brotherhood. No earthly bondage compares to the bondage of sin.

But we needn't diminish the sorrow of sin to see Christ exalted. No, my son. The more we acknowledge the bleakness and the stark divides of this world, the brighter the promise of unity in Christ shines.

You, Too, Sing America

Once, a colleague of mine asked me if it was hard to teach history at a classical school since much of our study focuses on the West.

"Is it weird when so many people who look like you are left out of the story?"

Honestly, it used to be. Classically educated myself, I always felt the absence of heroes and heroines who resembled me. The saying goes, "History is written by the victors." And the victors in the stories I learned in school were white westerners.

But I shrugged and smiled at her. "America is a really short story," I told her. "History is long. And people who look like me have had a huge hand in shaping it back when people who look like you were still considered the barbarians."

Learning history has given me a long view of the world. It has taught me that heroes are not without complexity, that bias impacts how we paint victors, and that we all tend to gravitate toward the stories we feel revolve around us. As a minority in this country, you'll find a lot of stories that *don't* include you. But if you look a little closer, you'll find that there are myriad stories of renown involving people who looked just like you.

No, America's founding fathers weren't actually as diverse as the cast of *Hamilton*, but your ancestors helped establish this country and were instrumental in the foundation of their own illustrious kingdoms back in the day.

Here and now, though, we really have come a long way in America.

Strides have been made in my own life that I hope will be reflected in yours, at the very least in how difficult conversations unfold among brothers and sisters of the faith. There have been and continue to be many strides made in terms of acknowledging the ways in which our ancestors and their sufferings contributed to the bedrock of the nation that we now dwell in. So many strides that make our votes and voices so important.

Your legacy is not just one writ in tears, but one writ with hard-fought victories. The sufferings of your ancestors have dignity because their pain has been dignified by our suffering Savior. Sometimes, being both black and American is complicated as we look at the historical landscape. Deciphering which of our community's blights result from systemic injustice and which stem from personal and generational responsibility is complicated. Knowing which political party has our best interest at heart on any given issue at hand is complicated.

Representation is complicated.

Seeing the full scope of history and inhabiting just a tiny sliver of it while dealing with the fallout of that sliver is complicated.

It's okay that it's complex. Because we have a Savior who sits with us in that complexity. And your identity in him supersedes that red, white, and blue flag every single time.

Love,

Mama

Ode to Langston

Dear Son,

Your daddy told me what your name would be two weeks after we started dating.

We were talking on the phone and he mentioned the most impactful professor he'd ever had: Walter Wynn Kenyon. Dr. Kenyon died before your daddy and I ever met, but his impact lives on through several little Wynns in and around the Jackson area. I could not be prouder to have you named after one of the very first men who discipled your father.

As I write this, your little brother is growing inside of me, and his name is meaningful to us in a different way.

An older woman at the grocery store once asked me if Langston was a family name.

It's not an uncommon question here in Mississippi, the land of double names for little girls and family surnames for little boys.

"He's named after my favorite author," I told her.

To which she responded, "Which one?"

You've got to love Mississippi, little one. It's grown on me because it is ripe with opportunities like that one: introducing a southern belle to Langston Hughes for the first time.

While little Langston's namesake wasn't a mentor of mine, his poetry has shaped me for a number of years. I can't begin to express what his words mean to me, but when it comes to explaining what it means to be both black and American, I have to try.

The miracle of Langston is that he somehow managed to be both painfully aware of the inequity of the country in which he was a citizen and doggedly hopeful that this inequity would someday be set to rights. He yearned for his personhood and dignity to be acknowledged, all the while showing that neither was dependent upon that acknowledgment.

And he proclaimed hope for his bright American future. No matter what. In *I, Too, Sing America*, he hums with a wink and a smirk, acknowledging that there is work to be done, but with the hope that it will be done.

He sings like his ancestors, belting Negro spirituals in the fields. I love the words of the old hymn:

I looked over Jordan and what did I see
Coming for to carry me home
A band of angels, coming after me
Coming for to carry me home

He sings in the tradition of those who hoped in Christ for ultimate deliverance. And he sings with the double meaning of those who used their songs to speak coded words about deliverance while held by the shackles of slavery. He sings in the tradition of people who have a long-term vision of meeting ultimate freedom at heaven's gates and a short-term grit to pursue freedom during their time here on earth. He sings in the tradition of the *already* and the *not yet.*

He inherited the undaunting hope of those who came before him.

In fact, Langston always seems hopeful, even when he's not.

Of all of the poet's beautiful pieces, *Song for a Dark Girl* has been a favorite of mine since I first discovered Langston.

It's jarring in its darkness. Even the bastion of optimism can't spit shine a lynching. The champion of winking and smirking waiting seems defeated in the face of such loss.

Though, the rhythm of the poem offers an evil smirk of its own. The repetition of the word *Dixie* and the jazz-laden meter are too upbeat for the dark words. Too light. Hughes's rhythm is a taunting reminder that lynchings were often a celebratory affair "way down South in Dixie." White families would bring a picnic lunch to watch the gnarly death of a black body. The juxtaposition in this poem brings light to the grotesque.

Its darkness is multi-layered, multi-faceted, and seemingly hopeless.

And yet.

The last two lines still sing to me in grief and in waiting. They're preceded by a bitterness that I have so often felt: "I asked the white Lord Jesus, what was the use of prayer." The distance there is palpable. Not only does Jesus seem far off from this particular situation, he's also part of the oppressive *other* ("the white Lord Jesus").

But there they stand, nonetheless: "Love is a naked shadow/On a gnarled and naked tree."

Many a scholar has tried to decipher their meaning because Hughes seems to mean something *beyond* the man on the tree. When I first read them, years ago, they settled in my mind and heart, gnawing at me. I came to the same conclusion as many others.

Because when I think of a naked shadow on a gnarled and naked tree, my mind jumps straight to Calvary. To a Savior who is not a blonde-haired, blue-eyed other, but a tan Jewish minority languishing on a cross. Suffering alienation, hostility, and isolation. And many think that's who Langston is pointing to as well.

In Langston's poem, the naked shadow is juxtaposed against the austere white Jesus. He paints Jesus black and compares the suffering he endured at the hands of evil men to the lynching that his black children often endured in the South. Even the phrase "cross roads" points boldly to the cross.

Here again, many different interpretations abound. Is Langston saying that, ultimately, love died that day? That the religious posturing of the Southerners who laughed merrily at a lynching meant that hope died on that crossroads tree as well?

Or does it mean that just as Christ once suffered, endured misunderstanding, faced dehumanization on a cross, and rose again in victory . . . so shall we?

Jesus is the God of the universe. The answer to his suffering is *right there*. He could've hopped down from that cross in an instant and demolished every single person who stood against him. But he stayed there instead. He suffered. And his suffering gives ours meaning.

No greater love has any man than the love of the naked shadow on that gnarled and naked tree.

And because of him, we fight. We cry out. We beat against the doors of heaven, aching for an answer, for reprieve.

And we wait in the ultimate hope that reprieve will come. Whether it be from the darkness within our own hearts or from the hatred that lies in the hearts of others.

That is contentment. Trust that, in our hardship, God has us right where he wants us. And hope that, in his lovingkindness, he will not ultimately keep us there.

This is what it has meant for us to be both black and American. This is what it means to be a citizen here on earth and a citizen in heaven.

My son, I want you to be shrewd, careful, and to guard your party affiliation carefully beneath the shadow of the cross. Donkeys and elephants be hanged. Because that's the only allegiance that offers a roadmap out of the mire of the political mess we've made.

Trust your mama. To borrow a motif from Langston, I've been climbing these stairs for a good bit longer than you have.

Love,

Mama

FIVE

You Are the Church

Dear Son,

You were born on the frozen tundra.

Not literally, but definitely in the mind of your Texan mama. 2016 found your father and me in Minneapolis, Minnesota, shoveling the driveway in order to make it to my prenatal appointments. You might have been born in the heat of summer, but most of my memories of carrying you are in the chill of my very first real winter. Back then, I thought that you would grow up a midwestern boy surrounded by snow flurries and four distinct seasons. I had no idea that we would make the decision to move to Mississippi shortly after you were born. Neither did I expect that the first winter I went back to work I would get the snow day that never arrived while teaching in Minneapolis.

The kids were pumped. No uniform, no scrambling to finish homework, no long-winded PowerPoint presentations!

Until Mrs. Holmes emailed them the assignments that they needed to complete by our next meeting. Then they remembered: snow days are a momentary reprieve, but once the snow melts there's going to be a reckoning.

C. S. Lewis uses the analogy of an almost endless winter to teach young children about the coming of the king. In his book *The Lion, the Witch, and the Wardrobe*, it's always winter and never Christmas until Aslan bursts back onto the scene, bringing with him the glorious festivities that have been lacking in the frozen tundra that was Narnia.

I look forward to reading you these stories someday and telling you about how, even during the seasons of snow, we are preparing for an eternal spring.

The parallel isn't exact, but I think about that Mississippi snow day every time the conversation of race and justice devolves into the proclamation that we need to "just preach the gospel." As the conversation continues to reach fever pitch, I hear a barrage of familiar phrases coming from my more conservative brethren: social justice is worldly and imprecise verbiage; racism is hatred, and the gospel fixes that; everyone sins, and there is no need to highlight the specific sins of specific people groups (unless it's time to rattle off statistics about abortion or drug busts in black communities).

And all of these tend to converge into that ultimate phrase: just preach the gospel.

It sounds so right! It's like waking up dreading school and then getting the email that lets you off the hook.

"I know you felt really uncomfortable with all this race talk, but it's all good. Just preach the gospel!"

We can heave a sigh of relief. God's got this.

Truly. He does.

The gospel is the ultimate answer to all of life's questions. Michael Horton describes it this way: "God's promise of a son who will crush the serpent's head, forgive the sins of his people, raise them from the dead, and give them everlasting life solely on the basis of his grace for the sake of Christ."

We who were once alienated from God have been ushered into the family of faith through the death of God's Son, not based on our merit (or melanin), but because of his grace.

My son, here is an important detail that you must never forget: our primary goal in this life is not to bring about racial reconciliation in the church. In fact, our primary goal isn't even to bring about justice here on earth. The ultimate justice has been dealt to Christ on the cross, accomplishing our reconciling in him.

As believers, we are absolutely in the business of spreading a message of reconciliation. But that reconciliation goes far beyond the scars accrued throughout America's spotty history of racial injustice. And so does our quest for racial justice.

Paul explains this ministry of reconciliation beautifully in 2 Corinthians 5, pointing out that we do not regard people according to their flesh but according to the new creation they are in Christ (2 Cor 5:17). Our ministry of reconciliation hinges on the truth Paul proclaims in this passage: "All this is from God, who through Christ reconciled us to himself and gave us the ministry of reconciliation; that is, in Christ God was reconciling the world to himself, not counting their trespasses against them, and entrusting to us the message of reconciliation" (2 Cor 5:18-19).

We are ambassadors not of the amount of melanin in our skin, but of the good news of Christ's redeeming work. *This* is the good news that we proclaim: we serve a God who is in the business of reconciling all that was lost in the Garden of Eden when our first parents sinned.

This message of reconciliation has to have implications for how believers relate to one another. We are united with bonds that are stronger than the familial bonds of our kinsmen (Mt 19:29). Our priorities are organized not around things of this world, but around another world entirely.

Yet the gospel we preach is a very specific message. It isn't all of the good things we're supposed to do. And we technically aren't just preaching the gospel when we talk about the implications of the gospel.

I want to be careful because there are two different ways we could be talking about the gospel. We are either talking about the actual message—the good news, the protoevangelium—or the covenant of grace that it entails. The former is God's fulfillment of the promise he made in Genesis 3:15. The latter involves the way that we live in light of that proclamation.

As you grow up, you will learn that your Christian brethren have a tendency to either use "the gospel" (the phrase, not the substance) as a catch-all for every good work Christians should be doing or as a silencer for anything too difficult to think about.

How many times do we mash the revelation of God's Word into pat slogans to attack the world's problems? "The gospel is the answer!" How conveniently the entire counsel of the Bible can be diminished to simple answers for our deepest problems—less like a textbook and more like the microwave instructions on a carton of ramen.

In a world full of complex beings, there are bound to be complex problems. As believers, we have been called to dwell in this world until Christ returns, spreading the message of the gospel in the hope that God will save sinners for his glory. Our most pressing issues have been laid at the foot of the cross.

Whatever struggles we face in this life pale in comparison to the glory that we have been promised in eternity. In our sinfulness, we deserved death, hell, and the grave. But "while we were still sinners, Christ died for us" (Rom 5:8). "For our sake he made him to be sin who knew no sin, so that in him we might become the righteousness of God" (2 Cor 5:21).

Now, those for whom Christ died are God's sons and daughters through faith (Gal 3:26). And he cares for us (1 Pet 5:7). He will never leave or forsake us (Heb 13:5). Even in moments where we feel most abandoned, he is near and he is at work (Ps 34:18; Rom 8:28). In the mire of our deepest regret, in the pit of our deepest longing, the gospel shines as our truest hope. We have been justified. We have been adopted. We are his.

Yes and amen. The gospel is the answer. You will get no argument from me on that point.

But . . . what exactly is the question?

You Have a Duty

The primary responsibility of the people of God is to preach the message of God.

As Jesus ascended into heaven, he gave his disciples pretty clear marching orders:

Then Jesus came to them and said, "All authority in heaven and on earth has been given to me. Therefore go and make disciples of all nations, baptizing them in the name of the Father and of the Son and of the Holy Spirit, and teaching them to obey everything I have commanded you. And surely I am with you always, to the very end of the age." (Mt 28:18-20 NIV)

Jesus said a lot more here than "just preach the gospel."

He gave a specific, authoritative command to *make disciples*—enter into meaningful relationships where the goal is to teach and admonish with the Word of God, teaching *all* that he has *commanded* them.

The gospel isn't a command: it's news. And yet here, Jesus is speaking beyond the news of his death and resurrection and giving his disciples not only the permission, but also a command to do the same.

In the epistles that follow the four gospels, we get a play-by-play of exactly where this discipleship is to take place—the church—and what it is to look like. When sinners become saints welcomed into the covenant of grace, the implications of the gospel get real, and Paul certainly preached them. The entire first half of Ephesians unpacks the gospel and the spiritual implications thereof, while the second half tells us what we are to do in light of that first half: walk in love (Eph 5:2).

And that love looks like doing *more* than just preaching the gospel. It looks like applying the implications of that gospel to every area of our spiritual walk and relationships . . . even when saying "just preach the gospel" is a lot more convenient than the actual application.

You Aren't a Fixer Upper

We are uncomfortable with vulnerability.

We like to pretend that's not the case. Our Instagram feeds are swimming with fake approximations of it, but in reality what we love are quick fixes, easy answers, and simple people.

Wouldn't it be great if everyone came with a user manual?

We would never have to worry about sticking our foot in our mouths because we would have a rulebook. We wouldn't have to worry about things like awkward silences, hurt feelings, or bruised egos, because there would be a script. Is your wife struggling after a miscarriage? Turn to page 519. Are you single and discouraged with the wait? Page 59.

Alas, no such rulebook exists. People are complicated creatures. And why shouldn't they be? They are made in the image of the most complex being in existence—the triune Creator of the universe. God reveals himself to us in his Word, but even that is just a small snippet of who he actually is!

This aversion to vulnerability extends far outside of the bounds of the church. It lurks everywhere. We are people who are only comfortable with anecdotal intimacy: you can only be vulnerable with me if you can express whatever problem you're handling with a solution. We want neat and tidy stories, like *Aesop's Fables*.

We have become so frightened by our culture where emotionalism reigns supreme that we are uncomfortable with any displays of emotion that aren't immediately followed by a fix. We want facts over feelings, answers over questions, and strength over honesty, and we could not care less about unique experiences.

Enter you, little boy, and your brown skin along with all of the complexity that it brings. Someone comfortable with the quiet space of learning to know another would welcome a relationship where you could unfold your heart about your identity and ethnicity, all the while striving to bring it under submission to the truth of God's Word. However, others who prefer simple fixes over your complications will find your brown skin to be an inconvenience they would rather overlook.

Enter the mantra "just preach the gospel," and you have a recipe for a guilt trip. Because that's what you're supposed to be doing, right? You are never supposed to deviate from that biblical script.

True enough, in a very real sense. But that script extends far beyond those four words. It is fully capable of diving deep and staying under without coming up for air. Not only is the Word of God (what people sometimes mean when they say "the gospel") enough, it's the only truth that gives our lives on this earth any real meaning. But saying "the gospel is enough" is not sufficient. Sure, it saves a lot of time and turns the Bible into a handy dandy, people-fixing manual. But it's not enough.

You see, son, when it comes to race, "just preach the gospel" often means "just shut up." Just tell people that Christ died to save sinners, and the race stuff will take care of itself. In Joel McDurmon's book, *The Problem of Slavery in Christian America*, we get an excellent example of how "just preach the gospel" can be misused:

When Unitarian minister William Furness preached his first antislavery sermon in 1839, some wealthy members of his Philadelphia church sitting before him held investments in southern

> slavery, in one case between 200-300 slaves. After his sermon,
> he received ugly notes inquiring how long he intended to
> preach such obnoxious doctrines, and that he would be better
> off to 'preach nothing else but Christ and him crucified.' As
> he continued, members left and others threatened to withhold
> crucial funds.

Just preach Christ and him crucified. Don't talk about how my
worldview should change as my mind is renewed (Rom 12:1-2). Stick
to the gospel.

This is how a nation that embraced the Great Awakening could
embrace slavery at the exact same time: give me that spiritual experience that *absolutely wrecks me* while I stand in the pew but doesn't
really touch my idol of comfort when I leave the church.

I know, son. Shots fired. We're not supposed to talk about the
Great Awakening like that. But how else can we reconcile a so-called
revival that left so many saved brethren languishing in chains? People
are people, and we will always find a way to embrace the parts of
biblical truth that we like while maintaining our cherished idols.

But the Spirit is the Spirit. And when he comes in power, he reveals to us that our only hope in this fallen world is to surrender *every*
area of our lives to the God of the universe. Even those closest to our
comfort. For John Newton, it meant surrendering the lucrative enterprise of the transatlantic slave trade. For you and me, it could be
something as simple as exercising patience with fallen people.

For God so loved the world that he gave his only begotten Son
(Jn 3:16), not for a quick death on the cross immediately followed
by Christ's ascension back into heaven, but for years of intensive

ministry with broken people. If anyone understands the complexity of humankind, it is Christ himself who lived as a man and is intimately acquainted with our struggles (Heb 4:15).

Our Savior is not merely sympathetic. He is empathetic. He did not shake his head on the sidelines merely imagining what we were going through—he lived it, complete with a painful death in our stead.

So you and I should be patient with brethren who are impatient with the complexity of our skin tone and history. But we also have the recourse to call them to be patient with us as well.

Love,

Mama

SIX

You Are More Than Your Ethnicity

Dear Son,

Something I learned very early on in my tenure as a black pastor's kid at majority white churches was that my skin made people uncomfortable.

I can't predict your experience perfectly, but I know that someday you will likely know what I mean.

It's not that people avoided me—they didn't—but they definitely avoided any mention of my skin. I'm sure they saw it as the polite thing to do. I am, after all, more than my skin tone. But they avoided speaking of it in that awkward way people avoid speaking about a deformity. Think, "That Jasmine sure is nice. She's much more than the third eye in the center of her forehead—just don't look at it."

Race and ethnicity are such huge topics that they can, of course, be daunting. And when it comes to tackling them in a meaningful way, you might find that people choose to deflect instead, even when we're talking about racism.

"There will always be racism," they might say. "It will exist until Jesus comes back."

Does that mean we ignore the sin in this world?

Misogyny, misandry, and murder will exist until Christ's return. Christians still advocate against abuse, radical feminism, and abortion.

For instance, with abortion? We're fine with using not-technically-biblical terminology (like "pro-life") and more than willing to throw our hands up and say, "Wretches gonna wretch."

With racism (or prejudice), though, we're hesitant about using culturally specific language, because progressives use it. Cultural code is only fine if it comes from the right camp. Instead of reframing an important conversation that should be grounded in the gospel, we let culture define the terms.

We're children hiding under a blanket we've thrown over our heads.

Race, as we often use the term (not as in ethnicity or people group, like Revelation 7:9), is an evolutionary construct. Our country has a sordid history of using that construct to oppress image bearers. That history impacts the church, no matter what we call it. Biblically specific language is a must. Dismissing issues based solely on terminology isn't helpful.

There will be sin in this world until Jesus comes back. But that's not the message he left his disciples with. He left them with a responsibility to speak authoritatively into this sinful world and to bring a message of hope and transformation. That message won't be fully realized until he cracks the sky and comes again, but the glimpses we achieve only serve to remind us of what's coming in eternity.

The tension of the *already* and *not yet* is not an excuse to throw up our hands in laziness or despair. It is an invitation to trust God and act as though his will can be done on earth as it is in heaven, because we have the ultimate hope in knowing that it *will* be.

You Are Neither Jew nor Greek

When we talk about our identities, there are so many aspects that we can focus on.

It can become especially tricky when we're talking about ethnicity. Some will be quick to point out that "there is neither Jew nor Greek" (Gal 3:28), neglecting to understand the context of the passage that this verse is found in.

In Galatians, Paul is specifically (and justifiably) railing against the Judaizers, those who wished to add their own cultural trappings to the gospel message. They preached a message of the gospel *and* circumcision, elevating their Jewish customs above mere Gentile conversion. Paul's aim in this epistle is to put these culture idolaters squarely back in their place.

And we commend him for that.

But if Paul's aim was to erase all distinctions, then he was a gigantic hypocrite.

The same man who penned Galatians 3:28 also wrote exhorting slaves and their masters (Eph 6:5-9), Jews and Greeks (1 Cor 9:19-23), and males and females (Titus 2).

You're two years old now and far too young to understand the implications of these verses (or sit still long enough for me to dissect them), but I want to teach you to master them because, as a black man growing up in majority-white Christian context, you're going to need them.

We know that there are differences and distinctions in each of these categories. While it's fun to be obtuse when we don't want to have a difficult conversation about race and identity, we must admit that Paul isn't using Galatians to argue that we shouldn't "see color." He's saying that, *no matter who we are,* slave or free, male or female, Jew or Greek, if we are in Christ, we are siblings who stand on equal footing before the cross.

That is really good news.

And it is that news that frees us to acknowledge those other categories of identity in submission to Christ.

YOUR ETHNICITY MATTERS

When I look at you, little boy, I see countless conversations that you might have that will caution you against making your skin preeminent. People will talk to you like being a Christian means that you are no longer black or that if you are it doesn't matter.

"Doesn't matter" is a tricky phrase. In one sense, it's accurate. Your ethnicity does not change your standing before a holy God—not an iota. You are still a little sinner in need of matchless grace. Your melanin makes you no more or less so.

In an entirely different sense, though, God made you an individual with a story to tell. And ever since your mama was an eight-year-old girl hoarding notebooks, she has *loved* to tell a good story.

You love to hear a good story too.

I love the way you climb onto the couch asking, "Sit with me?" (which means you want to sit with me—pronouns are hard) and thrust a book into my face. I hope that you will graduate from colorful, glossy pages with sing-songy rhymes to the onion skin pages of the Bible, but also to the myriad works of literature that made your mama choose to be an English major in college.

I hope you'll be captivated by the beautiful stories that God's common grace allows his image bearers to tell, because our God is a storytelling God. One need only look into the pages of his Word to see that narrative plays an integral part in his unfolding revelation.

And your ethnicity is part of your narrative, like the Moabite woman who laid down on the threshing room floor, or the Canaanite woman who saved two Jewish spies, or the flesh-wrapped Son of God who was Jewish because God chose his family tree.

The Bible is full of ethnicity, from the parents of every ethnicity imaginable in Genesis to the union of every ethnicity imaginable in Revelation. It's a part of God's story and it's a part of yours.

My little brown-skinned boy, you can't understand a word of this right now, but I hope you will in time: your skin color will never change your status before Jesus. Full stop. And it's part of his glorious plan in the unfolding of your story all the same.

You Can Stay in Uncomfortable Places

The gospel does not compel us to have a stiff upper lip, but to cling to a Savior who bears our burdens and a church that does the same (Ps 55:22; Gal 6:2). Yes, we believe the best, but we also confront (1 Cor 13:7; Mt 18:15-20). We are co-laborers whose bonds go a lot deeper than hard conversations. So let's have them instead of having dialogues about how to shut up the dialogue.

Someday, we'll worship together without baggage. Until that heavenly day, false reprieves from the discomfort of this issue only serve to pile up the mountain of homework we have to do to learn how to love the body well (Jn 13:34-35).

My dear boy, empathy takes time. It demands a listening ear. It requires treating people not like cars with manuals stuffed in the dash, but like, well, people. It takes not just spouting off, "The gospel is enough!," but preaching the gospel and being willing to apply it to specific situations, even when it takes more time than tossing out a slogan and moving right along.

It takes being willing to sit in those vulnerable moments for a beat and not defensively shouting, "But what do you want from me? How can I fix it?" Because you can't fix this world we live in—only God can. And he is working on his own timetable. Living in the *already* and *not yet* should give us infinite patience to parse out these things, because we literally have all of eternity to do so. There is no rush.

So it's okay to be broken for longer than the five minutes it takes someone to give you a pat answer to your suffering. There is space in God's plan for mourning, even when there isn't space in our comfort zones (Rom 12:15). The power of his Word is so much bigger than a few pat answers. It can carry every aspect of a life lived out for his glory (2 Tim 3:16; Heb 4:12). And that is a huge part of what the body of Christ is all about.

Love,

Mama

It's Okay to Be Offended

Dear Son,

Inevitably, conversations with proclaimers of "Just preach the gospel" will turn to an exasperated eye roll about the *perceived* sufferings of black Americans in the church. "You're there to worship. The church isn't about making you comfortable."

Amen. Nor is it about the comfort of our white brethren. If we're passing around big boy pants, everybody should get a pair.

I say this because, as a black young woman in predominantly white spaces, I was often tempted to stifle my concerns *because* they were in the minority. Under the guise of promoting peace, I embraced an unhealthy silence about how I felt when certain comments were made or certain statements went unchallenged. I thought that in order to be accepted by my peers, I needed to keep a stiff upper lip. If I wanted to be in, I had to leave my emotions out.

Some of the comments I ignored were innocuous. I was the brown-skinned girl who stuck out like a sore thumb in a sea of white, Reformed faces. I got used to answering questions about my hair ("Can I touch it?"), my skin ("Do you have to wear sunscreen?"), and my views ("Is this racist?"). But some of them were so very hurtful and made me feel *other*. Like when people would make comments about how hard it would be for me to find a white husband who "wouldn't mind" marrying a black woman, or what an exceptional prospect I was "for a black woman." One of the first guys I ever liked told me he'd "always wanted to know what it would be like to kiss a black girl," as though the experience were one to be crossed off a bucket list.

I should have spoken up, but, honestly, I didn't have the agency to do so. I didn't understand that these hurtful comments were coming from a deep place of ignorance because I was ignorant as well. Part of the reason why I'm teaching you their history isn't so you can walk around perpetually offended, but so you can calmly voice things that stop these cycles of ignorance.

I'm not advocating that we pretend not to be offended or confused when we are. The stiff-upper-lip mentality that's often advocated for offended minorities is pushed more out of majority comfort than actual biblical truth. Yes, as believers, sometimes we will be called to suffering, but the Word, church history, and our nation's history are full of examples of enduring that suffering while still proclaiming God's truth, one's personal dignity, and the need for change. Similarly, silencing white brethren for the sake of minority comfort is not a dialogue, but a dictatorship.

There is nuance to be had here. And that nuance cannot be captured in simple terminology that has often turned totalitarian: "Just preach the gospel, but not its implications. Or you love your skin more than you love Jesus." I can be offended that you're "bringing race into the conversation," but you can't be offended by that big burden you're lugging around on your back, even though I'm supposed to be helping you bear it (Gal 6:2).

Love,
Mama

SEVEN

You Are a Brother

Dear Son,

You could not have been more excited to meet your little brother when I was pregnant.

I'm sure you didn't fully understand the ramifications of my growing belly and burgeoning fatigue, but you adore all things baby. Twice a week, when I take you to the daycare at my school, you fixate on all the sweet little babies in your class trying to see to their every need. When I took you to the chiropractor during my pregnancy, you sat vigil by my side throwing your arm over my stomach and proclaiming a possessive, "Mine" when the doctor got a little too close to baby.

I cannot wait to see you and sweet Langston playing together. And though I write these letters mostly to you because you are the boy that I have seen day in and day out, the spirit of them is for both of you—that you would *both* know your mother's heart for you in these tense times and that your mother's heart would reflect the heart of your Father in heaven.

Because ultimately, my sweet boy, as much as your heavenly Father loves the both of you and as much as our earthly familial bonds bind our hearts together, you are knit into a much broader story.

Your brotherhood has eternal ramifications.

YOU ARE A BROTHER-MAN

I am used to being the only black woman in the room.

Part of it stems from the way that I was raised. Your pappy pastored more than one predominantly white church during my childhood. Before your uncle and I became homeschoolers, we went to a predominantly white private school where I was, more often than not, the lone brown face in the classroom.

My running joke as a teenager was, "That black friend every white person I know talks about? She's me."

It was funny because it was true.

And sometimes, it *wasn't* funny because it was true.

There are things about blackness and brotherhood that you will have to learn from your father, but one hilarious aspect I can't wait for you to pick up is that nod.

That signature, almost imperceptible tilt of your head when you see another black face in the crowd.

I remember asking your pappy once if he just knew a lot of black folks around Houston. He laughed and shook his head. "No, baby, that just means . . . it's like hi."

I observed the nods many times growing up. Sometimes I asked outright about them, but other times I just absorbed them.

Another instance I remember is asking your gram once, "Mommy, when Aunt Pam says, 'BB and 'em,' is that like saying 'BB and *them?*'"

Something I soaked in all on my own was the world-weary nod, the labored sigh, and the *giiiiiiiiirl*—that is the brown girl's equivalent of the stereotypical white girl's "I can't even."

In spite of the fact that I was raised in a predominantly white subculture and endured endless grief from my cousins for talking and acting white, it was impossible for me to grow up divorced from black culture. And not just because I have black parents.

You see, regardless of what your father and I teach you about your heritage, when you walk out into the world you will do so as a black man. That is how people will perceive you. Whether or not you are aware of the history harbored in your brown skin, others will be. And while you might escape the affectations of African American subculture, you won't escape the ramifications of our historical moment. You are a black man, my son. And when other black men see you, they'll automatically see a brother.

YOU HAVE A BLACK FAMILY

You cannot look around the internet long without hearing that the black family is in crisis. Rates of fatherlessness, crime statistics, and trauma abound. As we've discussed, though the source of these numbers is complex, their complexity is usually flattened to make the case that the black community is in trouble. And while the church often says that the answer is Jesus, there are shockingly few people willing to show us exactly what that looks like in the face of brokenness.

You have the same blessing that I grew up with: two loving, Christian parents who are raising you in a traditional family.

But you're also reaping the blessings of your father before you in spite of the fact that those statistics about fatherlessness are a very real part of his own life.

I am not going to sit here and tell you that your daddy stared potential father wounds in the face and came away unscathed, because that would be a lie. But I will tell you that the people he refers to as his parents—his mother, his aunts, and his grandmother—raised him to be a beautiful man of God.

What I love about your nana and aunties is the fact that their sense of community extended beyond the four walls of their own homes and into the neighborhood. I love the sense of ownership they take over not just raising their own children, but also raising the entire Jones brood by lending a helping hand and a loving word whenever they could. I love that, when you visit your grandma in her tiny town of 800, you can literally walk from house to house on her block, knock on the door, and meet a family member who couldn't be happier to see you.

I love these black women and the vibrant community of matriarchs who will lay down their lives for the children in their care. And while absentee fatherhood is never something to celebrate, I rejoice in the fact that black women have tenaciously taken the helm when it comes to the formation of young black men. Your daddy is living proof that they can do so well.

You Are a Spiritual Brother

Son, the bonds of your family are strong. On my side, you have two grandparents, an aunt, and an entire tribe of uncles who adore you.

On your daddy's side, you have a number of great aunts, a great-grandmother, and a nana who will lay down their lives for you.

But beyond that, you have the body of Christ.

You are a brother, not only to your kinsmen "according to the flesh" (Rom 9:3), but also to the body that features every tribe, tongue, and nation that God has created (Rev 7:9).

When I think of your duty of brotherhood, I'm reminded of the apostle Paul, a "Hebrew among Hebrews" (Phil 3:5). While a well-respected Pharisee with a heart for his people, he was called to ministry among the Gentiles in spite of his own desires. He didn't *lose* his Jewishness in this ministry. On the contrary, he referenced it quite often in his epistles to drive home the point of the God who was knocking down ethnic barriers to bring the good news. He used his Jewish ethnicity to establish his authority among his kinsmen, but kept it in subjection to his Christian faith, which formed his primary identity (1 Cor 9:20).

His conversion did not erase his bond with his Jewish brethren. In fact, it made him even *more* anxious to see his kinsmen realize the depth of the promise given to Abraham (Rom 9:6-8). But his link to the Jewish people became secondary to his link to the most high God through the family of faith.

In Paul, we do not see a Jew who pretended to be a Gentile, giving up his heritage to further the gospel of Christ. We see a Jew who was born so on purpose by God's providential plan, a man whose Jewishness came into play *throughout* that plan.

It's mind-blowing, really. Our God is so wise. He created each and every one of his children with a unique cultural backstory that he weaves into his plan for our conversion *and* for the furtherance of the gospel.

Your cultural brotherhood is valid.

As long as it is in service of your spiritual brotherhood.

You Are a Good Brother

I want you to be a good brother in the faith just as I desire for you to be a good brother to Langston and any other children who may enter this household.

I desire for you to be a leader among your spiritual siblings, able to use your words in ways that build up the family of faith and bring honor to your Father in heaven.

I want you to understand the value of brotherly exhortation.

Exhortation is a booming business right now. As a young Christian man, I want you to be careful that you're sincerely seeking to build up the body rather than speaking out for clicks, controversy, or name recognition. It will be a hard balance to strike. Speaking boldly is bound to garner attention, but I hope you shepherd that attention with integrity.

Your mama is still walking that tightrope.

For me, exhortation is inexorably linked to empathy. To incite or encourage people, we must meet them at the point of their deepest need. We know their deepest need is Jesus. And that's our deepest need as well. So we always have something in common with the people we seek to exhort.

As believers, exhortation does come from a place of authority, but less from our own personal authority than from that of God's Word, which we wield with fear and trembling. In order to be truly encouraging to others, we must become like Paul who determined to know nothing but Christ crucified. We have to remove ulterior motives from our encouragement. We must encourage with love, not from the deeds of the flesh Paul mentions in Galatians 5.

You Are a Mediator

We may think about fleshly deeds as sexual immorality and idolatry, which might be easy enough for us to flee in our minds. But there are some deeds that crouch at the door of exhortation more than others: enmity, strife, jealousy, fits of anger, rivalry, dissensions, and divisions.

These often lead to downfalls in the form of personal vendettas, a love of drama, arguing for argument's sake, jealousy over the platform of someone we feel is undeserving, anger that causes us to be quick to speak and slow to listen, rivalries with siblings in the Lord, stirring up controversy, or dividing over non-essential issues of the faith.

The fruit of the Spirit, however, should be present in our exhortation: love, joy, peace, patience, kindness, goodness, faithfulness, gentleness, and self-control.

It's a love that boldly steps into an uncomfortable conversation grounded firmly in the kinship that we have in Christ Jesus. We all want the triumphal entry kind of love, but very few of us are willing to display the love of the cross.

We can extend this love not only to our own kinsmen according to the flesh, but also to our kinsmen according to the Spirit. In fact, those Spirit kinsmen should come first. But when we see members of both groups struggling to communicate with one another, it should be our duty and delight as brothers to both groups to mediate as lovingly as we possibly can.

Mediate for misunderstood black women. Mediate for downtrodden black men. Mediate for oft-forgotten minorities of other ethnicities. Mediate for white brethren. Mediate in the steps of your heavenly mediator, the big brother whose love for his family is the example we're all out to follow.

Love,

Mama

EIGHT

Be a Good Brother to the Sisters

Dear Son,

Right after we got married your daddy told me, "Seriously. Every time we're out, you're complimenting a sister."

You will soon learn that *sister* is a term that black folks use for any other black woman, along with *brother* for any black man. And your daddy was right. Every time I see a beautiful black woman, I go out of my way to tell her she's killing it.

"I'm trying to start a revolution," I teased him, a twinkle in my eyes.

I was just joking. Kind of.

You see, there's a big difference between being a black woman in the evangelical spheres that I'm writing to you about and being a black man. Outside of my desire for you to know and love Christ deeply, to serve the local body without reservation, and to spread the gospel to make Jesus known, I desire for you to be the type of young man who is a breath of fresh air to a black Christian woman.

The best example I can think of is the time that one of my friends—a young black man—posted a question on Facebook asking, "Black men: what is your favorite (non-physical) thing about black women?" I clicked the comments expecting to find everything but constructive answers to that question. A number of black men began responding to the question with positive comments about black women, some of them even acknowledging that they were often less than supportive of their black sisters in Christ. But predictably, the majority of the responses were a mix of confusion and annoyance:

"Why are you asking this question?"

"Why are you only asking black men?"

"Would it be okay if we asked the same question about white women?"

"Why does everything have to be about race?"

It was clear to me that the people commenting did not understand why black womanhood needs affirming. Certainly, there are times and places to affirm all women and anyone may do so, but a black man affirming non-physical attributes of black women is a special thing. And history tells us why.

It's not that I don't understand the origin of these questions. I do. If you've never been black in America or taken the time to learn about that experience, there are some important details that you might have glossed over in history class.

I'm not talking about *ethnic gnosticism* (a phrase coined by a pastor I know fairly well . . . hi, Dad), which is "a secret knowledge that only ethnic minorities can possess." No, this knowledge is free, and anyone with an active mind and an empathetic heart has the freedom to attain it. Unfortunately, a lot of the comments on my friend's status stemmed from ignorance. And I don't throw that word around lightly.

For me, *ignorance* immediately conjures up an image of condescension and cattiness about the speaker. The truth is I'm ignorant of a lot of things, like the customs of Southeast Asia, the nuances of Hinduism, and the intricacies of Australia's history. But when it comes to matters of race, the label of "ignorance" is stigmatized. All of us want to be seen as self aware and well educated about race, but we also demand simple answers within broad categories.

And these two desires war with each other.

You Will Know More

Our nation has a history that resists simplicity, especially when it comes to the ways it quite literally commodified black bodies via the slave trade. America placed a numeric value not only on the labor black people could provide, but also on their forms. Black men and women were seen as property.

In *The Problem of Slavery in Christian America*, Joel McDurmon points out that, as far back as the late seventeenth century, legislation protected white masters who fathered children with their slaves. Under British Common Law, the child of the master took on the master's status (free), which meant that the master was obligated to that child in the same way he was to a "fully white" child. In America, the child took on the mother's status (slave), leaving a father free from owning any responsibility toward his offspring.

Once slavery was abolished, this stigma did not immediately disappear.

Free black women stepped into a society that had busied itself shaping a set of Victorian values while they were hard at work in the fields. Femininity had been defined in their absence. Purity became the female stronghold, but black women were not considered pure. Like their black male counterparts, they were overly sexualized, but rather than being thought of as predatorial they were seen as animalistic prey.

In her book *The Warmth of Other Suns*, Isabel Wilkerson points out the irony that a black man could be lynched for looking at a white woman whereas white men suffered little stigma for bedding a black woman, provided he wasn't trying to marry her. A popular saying arose amidst the sexual abuse experienced by black women in the South: "No white man wanted to die before bedding a black woman."

You Will Touch Old Wounds

Times have changed, undoubtedly. I am not claiming to have gone through the same harrowing life as my ancestors. Nor am I claiming that the majority of my white brothers and sisters in the Lord systematically assent to the lies of these narratives—not by a long shot. But our mindsets are touched by this history, and unearthing the social backdrops that have shaped us will help renew our minds.

I know well the history of sexualizing and devaluing black women in this country because I've heard its remnants in words spoken directly to me.

Before I met your daddy, I sometimes felt like an outsider in conversations about purity and worth. People made comments about how hard it would be for me to find a black husband (since most white men wouldn't want a black wife). I even had one woman go out of her way to tell me that she "wouldn't mind" her son marrying me, because even though I'm a black girl, I have other merits. One of the first guys I ever liked had a long list of things he couldn't wait to do with me because he'd never done them "with a black girl." (His list was not fulfilled with me, notably.)

When I describe the historical context for these kinds of remarks, I often receive a pat answer in response: "We're all one race—the human race. Color doesn't matter." I understand that answer. It seems so simple, so biblical! After all, there is neither Jew nor Greek (Gal 3:28), and race is a social construct, not an anthropological one.

But we live within social constructs so we have to do the hard work of understanding them before we can simply dismiss them. Instead of saying, "Race is just a social construct," we might say instead, "Let's be honest about how this social construct has shaped a lot of your life. Let's combat those thoughts with biblical truth. Let's affirm the heritage God gave you on purpose. Let's sit in an uncomfortable moment for a bit longer than a pat answer allows."

So here's your mama, sitting and talking to you about the young black women you're called to be a brother to. Pay special attention to caring for young, single, black women, because that was my loneliest season in the church.

Love Black Women

Changing the narrative that has so often described black women as worthless, oversexualized, loud-mouthed, and angry, we can praise black women as strong, loyal, and fiercely protective.

Generalizations? Absolutely. This timid black girl will be the first to tell you that my perceived "strength" is sometimes just a mask for my brokenness. But each of those words—strong, loyal, protective—has a connection to the history that has shaped me.

When we talk about womanhood—when we talk about stereotypes —I want to remind you every once in a while how those stereotypes have uniquely shaped me as a black woman. When I do, I'm not "making everything about race." Rest assured, I want to make everything about Jesus.

But part of my testimony means retelling the ways that his love is healing what our society has rent asunder. It's part of my story. And we're all about storytelling here.

Love,
Mama

Be an Advocate

Dear Son,

As I've told you many times, your birth was one of the most beautiful days of my life.

I've already talked about the tears, about taking you home for the first time, about our intense love and hope for your life. But your birth wasn't just the day that *you* came into this world—it was also the beginning of my quest to become a better advocate for myself.

Your mama was a shy child. Gram used to have to force me to speak up while ordering in restaurants, and Pappy encouraged me again and again to stick up for myself, but they also teased me about being a high-maintenance drama queen.

Which isn't false, at times. You definitely inherited your flair for the dramatic from me.

But eventually, I started to think that speaking up for myself only created drama and that advocacy was characteristic only of a high-maintenance person.

Until I became pregnant with you.

You see, black women are 300 times more likely to die in childbirth than any other ethnicity—and that's regardless of our socioeconomic status. I knew that in order to have the type of birth that I wanted, I was going to have to learn how to speak up. And I did. I left my original OB, went to a birth center, and made my needs known. Your birth was idyllic, and I learned something about myself: it is okay to speak up and, as a mama, I will *have* to speak up.

Moving to a state with twice the C-section rates as the one you were born in (Mississippi seems to be last in everything except for C-section rates) and black mother mortality rates that made my stomach turn, I knew I would have to advocate for my son and myself once again. And I have. I found my doctor after eavesdropping on a conversation at a coffee shop. I noticed two black healthcare professionals talking about how to give black mothers tools for successful nursing relationships with their babies, and I overcame every inch of introversion in my soul and marched right up to them.

"I'm a nursing mom," I told them (talking about you) and I got the doctor's number. I have a black, female obstetrician not because I wouldn't trust a white male to deliver Langston, but because she happens to be at the forefront of the birth advocacy I'm passionate about.

There I go again, talking about birth. By the time you read these words, you'll likely know how to roll your eyes and ignore your mama's passion for birth. But while my gateway to self-advocacy has been facing down systemic issues in the disparity of medical outcomes for black moms, yours might be any number of things.

And when it comes along, I want you to be ready to stand strong.

You know the angry black woman stereotype, of course.

While the angry black man stereotype might not be as well in-grained, it definitely exists. I will never forget the time your pappy objected to me going through the new body scanners at the airport. A TSA agent pulled me aside and asked me if I felt safe.

"He's my dad," I told her, visibly confused at how she could think that my big teddy bear of a father was a threat.

Little boy, when I think of the man that you'll become, I recognize that you won't be small. At this writing, you're not quite three years old, but we've already had to start buying 4T clothes. Every time I get an ultrasound, the sonographer remarks that Langston is going to have *long* legs, and I just have to laugh. My sons will have long *everything*.

You will be imposing not only because of your height (or the deep, rich voice I expect you to inherit from your daddy), but also because of the color of your skin. In a world where police officers have gunned down a little black boy with a toy gun because they confused him for an armed, adult, black man, I realize that your skin tone alone will be enough to cause some people to fear you.

There have been times when my own fear of being confused for an angry black woman has kept me from speaking up on my behalf. I have weighed the options again and again, worried that I will be labeled "difficult," "concerning," "scary," or, of course, "dramatic."

It used to be "common knowledge" in the medical community that black people did not feel pain in the same way as their white counter-parts. They were simply considered overly dramatic and expressive. Many black women have told stories of how doctors did not believe their symptoms, because they assumed their patient was overreacting.

I have literally been in the throes of labor pains apologizing for moaning in agony because I didn't want to be too much of an imposition.

That's a combination of my own personality, my upbringing, *and* my heritage.

Son, when I see elements of my personality in you, I fear for the area of self-advocacy, because you will have to contend with those three factors as well. Listen to me on that second factor: I want to raise you to know that speaking up is not an act of anger or aggression no matter the color of your skin, the timbre of your voice, or your gender. It is okay to say "ouch" when you are in pain.

I want you to be a reconciler: someone who, in light of the fact that Christ has reconciled us to the Father, seeks to reconcile with his brothers on earth. This doesn't mean being a pushover but doing the hard work of digging deep into relationships, which involves honesty and knowing when to overlook an offense and when to confront one. It also involves fighting for justice, even when it's awkward.

You Matter

Self-advocacy can also be difficult when you're in the minority. Why rock the boat when the majority is just fine?

I know I've already talked about birth, little boy, but bear with your mama as she gives you one more feminine example. Black women make up most of the buying power in the beauty industry, yet they lack representation. I can't buy makeup at the drugstore because most companies are only now getting the memo that black women come in a variety of shades. And not all of them are called "mocha."

When I voiced my frustration over generic foundation names ("mocha," "pecan," "almond"—"why are they always edible?"), a white acquaintance responded, "There are tons of things in nature that resemble brown skin. White skin is just . . . well, it's just flesh. There aren't a lot of ways to describe it."

"Sand, alabaster, snow, ivory, peach," I rattled off.

She smirked at me. "None of those describe my skin tone."

"Well, yeah," I told her. "But mocha doesn't describe mine either."

She paused, genuinely confused.

You see, for her, white skin was such a default that *nothing in nature* could possibly resemble it. My brown skin, however, could be easily described with a generic label.

(By the way, I think foundations should just be numbered to eliminate all of this foolishness.)

My sweet boy, while you might never stand in the makeup aisle searching for your shade among three brown colors in a sea of peaches and tans, you will know what it's like to be one of three black faces in a sea of white ones. And it may seem awkward to speak up for yourself.

What if they think you're too much? What if they think you're too sensitive? What if they just don't care?

Maybe they will think all of those things. But please do not let this stop you from kindly, gently, humbly, and forcefully making your case. Scripture commands brothers and sisters in the faith to bear one another's burdens (Gal 6:2). It is hard to bear your brother's burdens when he does not make them known.

You Will Be Misunderstood

It is also hard to care about the burdens that you don't understand.

You will have people in your life who don't wish to understand you. You will have people in your life who want you to play the martyr, forever sacrificing your own well-being and never receiving sacrifice from those who are called to do the same. You will have people in your life who take their own privileges for granted and expect you to suck it up when it comes to a deficit that doesn't impact them.

You will have people who consider themselves your allies until you make them uncomfortable.

You will have people who shame you, citing verses like Philippians 2 when it comes to sharing your offenses or needs ("he did not consider equality a thing to be grasped, and neither should you"), but acting more like Matthew 21 ("when your brother offends you, go to him, so here I am") when it comes to citing their own.

You will survive, dear one.

Your heart might be crushed, and it will hurt me so much to see. But I will always comfort you when you're wounded. I will encourage you to get out and try again. I will celebrate you when you find people who endeavor to meet you and labor with you to find common ground. I will fight with you to advocate in a way that honors God and your fellow man.

Remember the first scrape you ever got?

We were outside of school and you tripped and slid across the gravel. I ran to help you up, and you cried a bit as I dusted you off. My heart broke when you held up your arm and showed me the bloody little scrape.

"What can Mama do?" I asked you.

"I just want you to kiss it," you told me.

When I did, you grinned a mile wide and wiped your nose. "I feel better."

I wish it could always be that easy, my beautiful brown-skinned boy. But long after you've outgrown those kisses on your boo-boos, I will be here to help you do the hard work of nursing the wounds that your brothers and sisters in Christ will (many times, accidentally) deal you. And even when I'm not, you have a Father in heaven who can minister both to your wounds and the hearts of those who wound you.

Don't be afraid to fall.

Love,

Mama

The Time I Almost Unfollowed Someone on Twitter

Dear Son,

I almost unfollowed someone on Twitter today over a racially-charged tweet.

I don't know how relevant Twitter will be by the time you read this, but it's really relevant right now. It's where you go to see opinions marching across your screen in real time, inviting you to react with a simple push of a button. I follow more than 400 people, which means that I have 400 different opinions swirling on my timeline at any given moment, ready to be seen and responded to.

I followed the woman in question just a few days ago. We had interacted minimally, but I'd seen her tweets shared by mutual friends and I appreciated her balanced perspective on several issues. Granted, I hadn't seen many of her perspectives on race.

Last night, I did. A white man tweeted: "Dear white people—let's get this straight. You can't be victims of racism. Racism means that the whole culture, society, economy, and much of what is considered law is against you because of your race. All of those things support white people. So stop claiming it, ever. Period."

The only reason I saw the tweet was because the woman retweeted it with commentary—not concerning her own experiences of racism, but sharing the grotesque suffering she had endured as a child and into adulthood. Because she had suffered without being black, she surmised skin color wasn't a variable in the suffering of others. Basically, she was saying, "Stop playing your PC victim games, because *I'm* the victim!"

Son, I have to admit that my hand hovered over the unfollow button almost instantly. Her dismissiveness, her emotionally charged response, her pride in her own position, all of it irked me.

Of course, the man who wrote the tweet had shown all of the above for any white people who ever considered themselves the victims of classically defined racism. But I don't follow him. And, frankly, he wasn't being dismissive of my experience so he was easier for me to take.

If that sounds selfish to you, it's because I think it is, at least a little. Perhaps, a lot. But the goal of these letters is for me to be honest with you about what you might someday feel. And though you will always hear me say that glossing over the hurtful words of others—even when they don't hurt *you*—is tribalism and not justice, I'm still retraining my mind.

And in that process, I'm having to realize that everyone thinks their indignation is righteous. I do. The man who posted did. The woman who retweeted did. The mere act of feeling indignation does not make it righteous.

I also realized that we all scroll through Twitter not as emotionless robots, but as human beings with an intense array of emotions and a complex network of personal history, trauma, and worldview. Neither the woman nor I read that original tweet from a pure, un-biased standpoint. She didn't write her tweet devoid of emotion. I didn't read it devoid of emotion.

And regardless of the logic lacking in what she said—which had nothing to do with actual racism and everything to do with her own traumatic past—I had a choice to make. I could either see her as a hurting sister in Christ, a fellow image bearer, or dismiss her as an adversary who no longer had wisdom to speak into my life in *any* category because I perceived her to be in error regarding this one.

I did not unfollow her last night.

That's not to say that I won't unfollow her in the future, or at least mute her for a while. That's not to say that I won't struggle with feeling annoyed watching people talk past one another in the echo chamber that is Twitter. But this was last night's victory. It says nothing of how I'll fare in the days ahead.

For you, son, I hope that you will be able to separate people from their ideas and their ideas from their pain. I want you to be un-apologetic about truth in all of its absolutes and compassionate about the pain that often taints that truth. I want you to see hurting people before you see ideological adversaries. Before you move to looking for the chink in your opponent's ideological armor, I want you to see your opponent as a brother in need of embracing—vulnerable spots and all.

That's not to say you'll always be singing Kumbaya in a field of daisies. No matter how loving you strive to be, there will be moments when you have to speak unpopular truths that cannot be sugarcoated. And I don't want you to sugarcoat them. But I want you to speak them from a heart that prizes truth because it belongs to God, not because it dominates the opposition.

And maybe stay off Twitter? Or whatever equivalent exists when you grow up. It's hard to see people diluted to 288-character hot takes. But you can certainly try. I will too.

Love,

Mama

TEN

Be a Bridge

Dear Son,

One of my very first memories is the time I sprained my arm at daycare.

I was almost four years old. Your gram had just given birth to my little brother and had gone back to work, so I spent my days at a childcare center until it was time to start pre-K at Fort Bend Baptist Academy (with Mrs. Montgomery). I was the only black girl in class, and even though it was 1993, I was regularly bullied by the bigger white kids.

They used to call me "nigger monkey," and I would lash out, not knowing quite what the words meant, but understanding that they weren't kind. Gram says that every day when she picked me up from school, I was disheveled from fighting, and my teacher would tell her what a problem child I'd been. When we'd get in the car, I'd be anxious to talk about other things, skirting around the name-calling.

I was just a little girl, but I knew shame. I felt the ugliness in those words and I felt ugly because of them. I didn't tell Gram about them because I was ashamed of them. I was ashamed of me.

But one day, a bigger boy called me that name and chased me around the playground yelling threats. He was too big to fight the way I did the other kids, and I was terrified. I fell off the side of the playset and right onto my arm. I was in such a state when my mom came that the entire story poured out in tears.

Even the part about monkeys.

Here's the thing about Gram and Pappy, Wynn. They hardly ever took my side in a dispute. When I would come home railing about another child, the *very first thing* they would ask me is, "But what did you do?"

But this time, Gram didn't ask me any questions about what I had done. She was furious. She yelled at my daycare teacher and berated all of the mean little children. Then she took me by the hand that wasn't hurt, and we never *ever* went back to that daycare center.

That's the kind of love underneath every single thing I'm about to say in this letter. Never do I want you to subject yourself to the abuse of others. As long as you're my little boy, I will be your champion and your defender just like Gram was mine. And as you grow into manhood, I'll teach you how to stick up for yourself, and for others.

This letter is all about being a bridge and learning how to have profitable discussions about race and ethnicity. But if you're having a discussion with someone who refuses to listen—who wishes you bodily harm, who wants to humiliate you, belittle you, and shame you—you always have my permission to walk away. Don't cast your pearls before swine.

This letter is meant to help you navigate dealings with the people who actually want to have a conversation with you. Who may not say everything in exactly the right way all of the time, but who truly want to understand your point of view. This letter is to help you talk to people who will be patient with you as you try to process your emotions in a healthy way. It is for learning how to address things with those who desire unity, as I hope you will desire unity.

Face-to-face relationships will be an important part of this interaction. But if your world is anything like mine, the internet has become a central player in these dialogues. I want to give you three overarching principles that I think will apply well in both arenas: be transcendent, know when to walk away, and don't fear the gray.

Be Transcendent

Your daddy and I call ourselves *transcendent*. That might seem a bit arrogant if you don't realize that it's something we're constantly striving for, not something that we've achieved yet. We don't want our voices to fit neatly into the Rock 'Em Sock 'Em categories that are constantly making their rounds on social media. Instead, we want to speak out above the din, calling our brothers and sisters in Christ to a higher, biblical standard that makes them unafraid of admitting where the other side is right and pointing out where they are both wrong.

No one has to knock three times on our front door and say a password to be accepted into our family. All they have to do is love the Lord above all else. When they do, it opens us up to dialoguing about hard things while remaining committed enough to one another to donate a kidney, even if we don't see eye-to-eye.

It doesn't feel like we're asking too much (except maybe for the kidney part), but we are. In a time where people are much more comfortable drawing hard and fast lines in the sand, we want to examine these lines and make sure they line up with biblical boundaries. And when they don't, we're more than happy to Riverdance all over them.

We all like to feel that we belong.

As you know, I don't have an athletic bone in my body, but I love a good sports movie. It's the camaraderie of a scrappy little group banding together to defeat the odds. I love the idea of a tribe. (And if your daddy has his way, you'll understand all of that sports camaraderie on the basketball court.)

What I don't love is a clique.

Sometimes, I feel like the entire purpose of these conversations is to join the right clique and then spend the rest of time measuring applicants and puffing ourselves up when we find them wanting. We want an excuse to say, "You can't sit with us," instead of pulling out a chair and beginning a difficult conversation. We don't even want to learn how to *have* a difficult conversation. We just want to know how to shut one down.

I want you to transcend the cliques that we so eagerly gravitate toward and to share truth that doesn't neatly fit into our tribe's boxes because you're more interested in prizing the gospel than facilitating a peer group. That will mean disappointing people on all sides of this discussion, from those who want to make race ultimate to those who want to discount your unique struggles altogether. I want you to be transcendent and to know that your God is capable of turning hearts even when you're honest about complex truths.

For instance, I want you to acknowledge that victimology has gone too far in our culture. That identifying yourself solely by your status as a victim of racism is much too narrow a box. That you are actually *more* than a conqueror through Jesus Christ. That will make right wing folks cheer.

And then I want you to make some of those folks a bit uncomfortable by acknowledging *real* victims of racism, sexism, and abuse. I want you to confuse them by affirming that we are complex conquerors, that we conquer *in spite of* real and acknowledged hurt. That we can conquer even when we're honest about the pain. That there is *real pain* to conquer, and that we can't defeat it by pretending it doesn't exist.

Know When to Walk Away

I often think about that scene in *Beauty and the Beast* where Gaston rallies the townspeople. They were handing out library books and baguettes at the beginning of the movie, but he turns them into a frothing mob with pitchforks and torches by the end.

That's what it's like talking about racial reconciliation.

The stated goal is handholding, Kumbaya moments. The execution is a mob mentality.

Especially on the internet. With just a few clicks, a member of our tribe can rally us to swift and decisive action. We become judge, jury, and executioner based on a tweet, a blog post, or a single sermon. Suddenly, someone who we aren't in community with—who we didn't care a stitch about until we decided we disagreed with them— becomes our adversary. Just like that, confrontation is divorced from brotherhood and community.

And once we've tasted blood, we just can't stop. The pitchforks will not be put down until the beast is hurled from the side of the castle. No time to stop and think. No time to pray. No time to reconsider. And definitely never *any* chance that you could be wrong and need to apologize. Kill the beast.

What if, instead of running with the mob, one of the villagers had said, "Do we really even know this beast guy? Maybe we misunderstood him. Someone should have him over for dinner."

Okay, so that would have totally ruined the ending of the movie. But in real life? Rock star move.

I want you to be that rock star.

I want you to be the one who speaks calm into chaos. The one who pursues peace. The one who asks clarifying questions and seeks understanding. The one who will not rest until you can state your opponent's argument in terms so compassionate that you finally understand where they're coming from.

Again, I'm not talking about frothing racists here. I'm talking about the people who truly want to understand one another but have a hard time bridging the gap. I want you to stand in the gap for them. There may be times when you have to dust off your sandals and keep it moving, and I pray that you will have the wisdom to know when that is. When you run into the stone wall of indifference, mockery, or even violence, I want you to know that it's okay to walk away.

DON'T FEAR THE GRAY

The lack of transcendent thinking and the inability to reason well with opposing viewpoints are often the results of black-and-white thinking.

In the nineties, there were all of these intense worldview books and quizzes that told you exactly who you were based on your answers to a few critical questions. I loved the neat boxes and shiny rules that kept me from ever having to admit that the world can be a complex, scary place and that people are actually shockingly inconsistent.

The Bible gives us an absolute moral standard of life and practice. You will find no argument from me there. But there are places where Christians have superimposed cultural assumptions on the Bible and made *new* laws that keep them from having to wrestle with gray areas.

I hear your rebuttal: with racism, there *are no gray areas.* And you are absolutely right. With clearly defined racism, there are absolutely no gray areas. When one brother thinks he is superior to another brother simply because of the color of his skin, he is wrong. He is in sin.

But when it comes to actually parsing racial disparity and pinpointing racial and cultural superiority, I believe we have to tread carefully. I want you to be tenderhearted toward your white brother and sister in Christ, even when it seems they just *aren't getting* a concept like implicit bias. I want you to be tenderhearted toward your black brother and sister in Christ, even when it seems they are just *looking* for reasons to be offended.

I want you to see that 1 Corinthians 13 kind of love enables you to tread carefully in those muddy areas *even while* proclaiming the crystal-clear truth outside of them.

Be Willing to Learn

I also want you to learn—truly, holistically learn—the truth.

I want you to tirelessly seek it.

Which means I want you to read a lot.

I hope that, as you read these words, you have grown up in a house full of books. Currently, as I write this, I'm curled up in my bed next to four books I'm in the process of reading. The most overwhelming thing about seeking peace in this conversation is seeking to *learn*.

Now, there are those who might wrongly read into what I am saying, so I want you to hear me: I am not at all suggesting that the answer to American racism lies outside of the finished work of Christ Jesus. I am not suggesting that you have to have a sociology degree to know that you need to love your neighbor more and look out for your own interest less. That's basic Bible talk (Phil 2:4).

But something that I am learning now that I hope you learn early on is that the truth of the gospel is not threatened by the truth we learn elsewhere, but highlighted by it.

Put another way, understanding our social and historical context is not a threat to the gospel. God chose for us to serve him in this generation. Faithfully learning the details he's carefully woven together doesn't undermine the authority of the gospel. It magnifies the glory of the gospel.

I'm teaching ancient history right now, and one of the most astonishing witnesses of the truth of God's Word is the archaeological and historical record that supports exactly what it says. Similarly, in learning about the place we occupy in history, we magnify the fact that the gospel is applicable in even the most specific of circumstances. Learning those specifics equips us to better proclaim gospel truth.

I'm not going to go to a remote village in South America and start preaching in my language relating the gospel back to my own terminology. I'm going to learn as much as I can about the local cultural context so that I can respectfully apply gospel truth to those beloved souls.

OPERATE WITH LOVE

"If I speak in the tongues of men and of angels, but have not love, I am a noisy gong or a clanging cymbal" (1 Cor 13:1).

My son, regardless of how hard you try to be above reproach in this conversation, you will be labeled. It's just the nature of things. I've been called everything from a cultural Marxist to an Uncle Tom. And while both groups of name-callers will say that the other name is worse, the spirit behind both is sometimes exactly the same: I don't want to hear what you're saying so I will invalidate it with the pejorative of my choosing. Some people don't want a bridge because division is their bread and butter. They like battle lines because they're easier than clasping hands across the aisle. And they will *hate* you for trying to hold their hand.

But listen to your mama's voice. Because it will always tell you exactly who you are. And if the bullies ever get too loud and mean, I will march myself right up to the proverbial daycare and defend you from the rooftops.

Love,

Mama

How to Study and How to Talk

Dear Son,

One of the biggest roadblocks to having conversations about race and identity in evangelical spaces is a lack of education.

While people don't need an intensive education to understand the gospel of Christ (they can know *nothing* but Christ and him crucified), we do need education to understand where we fit into this world.

Now that I've carried your baby brother, I'm learning so much about birth. As you'll find out the older you get, your mama is a bit of a birth fanatic. I love to learn about how your little brother is growing inside of me, the part my body plays in his development, and how I can advocate for myself when it's time for delivery.

God didn't need my help to birth your baby brother. He sustained the little boy inside of me by his power alone. But he's given me the grace to be part of the process, and I want to learn as much as I can about it. Learning does not make me any less reliant on him and his will. In fact, it makes me more grateful than ever for his design.

Learning about the history of race in America is so worthwhile because you're going to hear it said over and over again—"Race is just a social construct."

But you'll also soon learn that some of the people who say this aren't interested in learning how it became a social construct, or *why* it's a social construct, or *who* invented the construct.

So as you learn, I want to give you some guidelines for conversing well.

DO: Be Excited About Learning New Things

One of my favorite teaching moments last year involved a three-hour class about the history of eugenics in America.

After picking up *War Against the Weak*, I was bursting to talk about everything I learned. Blessedly, I'm a teacher who generally has a captive audience twice a week. Because I was excited, they were excited. Because I was fascinated, they were fascinated. Our conversation was rich and multi-layered, and it all started with picking up a new book and strengthening my understanding of a concept.

You *should* be excited to learn new things, son. I want you to be bursting at the seams with fresh perspective.

DON'T: Learn Just Enough

When I was a teenager, I was notorious for reading a book just to prove someone wrong. I didn't learn for the sake of enjoyment or enrichment, but to crush my ideological opponent. Knowledge was a useful weapon to silence uncomfortable conversations, not a helpful tool for sharing an edifying truth. I didn't need to thoroughly understand a topic. No, just shut up and get to the part where I can win the debate.

By reading as an adversary, I wasn't looking for constructive conversations. I was looking to crush the opposition.

DO: Learn Enough to Re-Frame

Instead of learning just enough to shut down a conversation, learn enough to re-frame the conversation.

Oftentimes, we complain about other people's presuppositions, whether they're speaking from a place of privilege, assuming that you share their privilege, or making you cringe because you can't hear "privilege" without thinking of a Marxist worldview. My inclination in these situations was often to repeat my arguments over and over again (louder and louder), in spite of the fact that the person I was talking to just wasn't approaching the conversation from the same place I was. But the more I learn, the more I'm able to rephrase my point of view and discover the understandable parts of others'.

DON'T: Kill the Conversation

Another thing I used to do was learn new things in order to kill old conversations. Just give me the ideological zinger that will shut them up.

We love a good label. For most conservative evangelicals, the label is usually something like "feminist." Calling a woman a feminist in conservative Reformed land is like calling her Jezebel. The minute you've slapped that label on her, any further argument just solidifies the brazen hussy title. Other popular labels include "cultural Marxist," "liberal," and my personal favorite, "millennial."

DO: Learn Enough to Have a Nuanced Exchange

What if, instead of hurling around ideological labels, we took the time to define what we actually mean by them?

Take the term *feminist* again. It's not one that I apply to myself, but it's one that has been stapled to me every time I've offered pushback on a beloved female stereotype. The more I learn, however, the more I'm able to pause and examine feminism from several different angles (the historical one being my favorite) and explore exactly why the person I'm talking to has turned it into a pejorative.

The same goes for "cultural Marxist" or "liberal."

I can't really change the fact that I'm a millennial.

DON'T: Just Validate Your Preconceived Ideas

We know that God's Word is absolute truth. But sometimes, we confuse our particular understanding of God's Word with absolute truth.

We often supplement actual truth with our own cultural interpretations. It is okay to question those interpretations, and doing so is not automatically questioning God's Word but rather questioning our *understanding* of God's Word.

If God's Word is absolutely true, it can stand up to all of our investigations. It always has. It always will. Learning more about the world we live in will only enrich that truth. Especially if we uncover lies we used to hold dear.

DO: Challenge Your Biases

Read books about topics you've never even considered, yes. But also read books that challenge what you've always taken for granted.

The more I've done that, the more two things have happened: on the one hand, I've become more certain of some of my long-held beliefs. On the other, I've been able to free myself from some unnecessary long-held shame. It's been a journey, and I'm only getting started. Bolster your convictions by reading things that challenge them.

DON'T: Learn Enough Just to Give a Hot Take

I struggle to condense 300 pages of a meaty book into 280 characters.

And that's okay.

We live in an age where we're pressured to share our thoughts as we're thinking them. Reading broadly and deeply forces me to allow my thoughts to simmer and distill a little longer. That's good.

DO: Learn Enough to Realize You've Never Learned Enough

You will always be digging and learning.

Dig deep into a relationship with the person who you're engaging.

I'm a high school humanities teacher, not a PhD in either of the fields that I teach. I'm a professional of very small caliber. Even if I did someday reach PhD-level knowledge and credentials, there would always be someone a step ahead of me, someone who has known more far longer.

I'm trying to learn not in order to dominate, but to relate and reflect on God's truth.

DON'T: FALL FOR TRANSFER

This age-old propaganda technique rears its ugly head on the regular.

I describe it to my students as taking the qualities of something good and ascribing them to something questionable. That way, when we reject the questionable thing, we're seen as rejecting the good thing. Transfer relies heavily on definitions that have not been mutually agreed upon.

For instance, during World War II the positive quality many Americans agreed upon was that Americans and their values were superior to their opponents'. So any time an American flag loomed in the background of an ad, it unconsciously messaged, "You must agree with this text because it is the American way."

We still see "the American way" used as a catch-all for "the value system that I want you to submit to." During WWII, an ad might imply that if you didn't want to spend 10 percent of your income on war bonds, perhaps you hated America. Or your children. Or puppies. In this scenario, the merit of buying war bonds goes from being something that we can discuss as rational human beings to an unquestionable test of your devotion to the American value system.

In your scenario, you might be seen as questioning "the American way" when you bring up historical facts that make other people uncomfortable with their glossy view of American history. Remember, though: understanding our social and historical context is not a threat to the gospel. We are simply noting God's work in history.

DO: BE COUNTER-CULTURAL, BUT NOT JUST FOR COUNTER-CULTURE'S SAKE

This one is sneaky.

We all know we're supposed to be in the world and not of it. But that doesn't mean that we should use what's going on in the world as our barometer for what we're supposed to be doing (which would be the opposite).

Romans 1 tells us that there is truth to be found in the world. There are problems diagnosed by worldly people and movements that mirror the Bible's diagnoses. There is truth that the world stumbles upon that is actually part of the real story.

Just as we shouldn't get our identity from the world, we shouldn't draw our identity simply from being anti-world. Instead, we should get it from being pro-biblical. The antidote to our ungodly culture isn't an anti-venom, but an entirely set-apart medication.

An example of this would be to throw aside any mention of racism and justice as critical race theory and, therefore, anti-biblical jargon. Examine ideas for what they actually are. Don't cast them aside just because your enemies recognize their validity as well.

DON'T: BROAD-BRUSH

A well-known relative of transfer is broad-brushing.

As we've discussed, sticking people into neat, predetermined categories is an inevitable lure. Notice I did not say that *truth* is complicated. But the way that we understand and deliver the truth absolutely can be. It is so much easier to listen for buzzwords and lump people into broad, us-versus-them types of categories without further investigation than it is for us to take the time to get to know people and to walk with them in a relationship. To pull an example from the opposite side of the aisle, broad-brushing may be assuming that just because your white neighbors voted for a candidate who makes your brown skin crawl means they're racist. They've made a value decision that merits deeper investigation and writing them off is the easy way out.

DO: TELL YOUR STORY

Here's something that I have learned as a storyteller: my unique experiences as a black woman do not trump the power of the gospel. But neither does sharing those experiences as part of my story.

Telling my story as a black woman who grew up in predominantly white evangelical churches with a black pastor for a dad makes a lot of people uncomfortable. They're immediately on-guard about what they think I'm trying to get from them. They're afraid I want to exert some sort of power or superiority over them, perhaps as a "privileged victim." They're afraid I want them to blindly assent to my authoritative opinions on their level of privilege. They're afraid that I want to sneak attack them with Marxist ideology.

But what I want is for my siblings in Christ to consider that their experiences of evangelical culture are not universal. That our unique stories and experiences can serve to *amplify* the fact that Christ's saving power infiltrates every tribe, tongue, and nation. The fact that I'm a black woman isn't central to my identity as a Christian. But it is a facet of the way the Lord has made me, and it does impact aspects of my life that I have to wrestle with quite often in my earthly shell. It comes with immense blessings and difficult burdens.

We serve a burden-carrying Savior. He has called us to be burden-carrying siblings.

I want you to be equipped to share with others how they can help you shoulder those burdens that come with being a young black man in America. I also want you to be able to share their unique burdens with them. But first, we must become less afraid of the power of an unfamiliar story. And you get nowhere with people who refuse to do this.

DON'T: PLAY GOTCHA

Your dad always gets onto me for viewing conversations like a game of chess.

I tend to stay on my guard, measuring each and every word like I've just been read my Miranda rights. I'm listening carefully, too, ready to use my opponent's words in the same manner if push comes to shove. I'm ready and waiting to pounce on any ideological inconsistency, and when I find it, the first thing I want to do is say, "Gotcha!"

Here's the thing, though. Conversations are not chess games, and relationships aren't courtrooms. Waiting to pounce on the perfect gotcha opportunity makes for a very unsafe environment for learning and growing. People are never totally consistent, but those inconsistencies aren't opportunities for us to revel in an opportunity to win an argument. Rather, they are a chance for us to teach and then win our brothers, or be taught and won ourselves.

DO: Spot Hypocrisy

Growing up, I heard a lot of conversation about "the liberals" and their trigger-happy usage of the word *racism*. Those same people have become increasingly eager to fling it around themselves.

Fatigued by conversations of unconscious bias, they're retaliating with a game of, "I know you are but what am I?"

Someone brings up diversity in leadership? Racist. Someone brings up an aspect of cultural competency? Racist. Someone brings up ethnicity in a conversation? Racist.

While I realize that there is debate over the nature of this particular word, the way it's being flung about every time someone does something we disapprove of (from voting for the wrong candidate to asking us why all of our role models happen to be the same ethnicity) has turned it from a meaningful pointed charge to a meaningless barb thrown in a bar fight.

If we want measured speech from our ideological opponents, we should be willing to apply this same standard to ourselves. Like I tell my students, "He started it" doesn't really hold up with our Father in heaven. You should never accept it as an excuse for hypocrisy and inconsistency in yourself or in others.

DON'T: Read Uncharitably

A while ago, a prominent Christian leader posited that Christians should be theologically influenced by more than just white voices. I personally had a conversation with several people who read her tweet and saw what I did not see:

"She's obviously saying that our primary metric for choosing an author should be skin tone!"

"She thinks we shouldn't read any white authors!"

What she actually said was that we should read *more* than white authors, which is a conversation worth having. But it's impossible to have when we're reading things that have been written in the invisible ink of our assumptions.

We all read with a certain lens, son. You and I are completely capable of doing the same. We need to surround ourselves with people who are cognizant of this fact and actively working against it, not people who are content to believe the worst of anyone who hasn't pledged fealty to our ideological idols.

DON'T: MOVE THE GOALPOSTS

Lastly, you want to beware of aligning yourself with any tribe that constantly moves the goalposts.

If you see someone railing against transfer, broad-brushing, or story-silencing in another camp, watch and see if they're equally critical of their own bedfellows.

It's a hard thing to do, and no one does it perfectly. I've found myself more willing to call out the sins that I grew up silent about than the sins that haven't hurt me as much. And I don't think I'm alone in this tendency.

It is natural to care more about the things that affect us than those that affect other people. What you want to see, though, is people who are self-consciously battling against this urge.

Now here's what I don't want you to mistake for ideological consistency: self-flagellation and deprecation that takes the focus off of the gospel and puts it on signaling to the world just how aware we are of our own tendency toward sin. It's okay to remind others that you are the chief among sinners every once in a while, but you've replaced a gospel focus with self-focus if you're more concerned with proving that point than applying the truth of the gospel to the hurting world around you.

I also don't want you to be so focused on how marginalized you are that you lose sight of the gospel. We see this in black brothers and sisters who claim to be tired of the victim mentality of the liberal tribe (often with validity), but tout their own conservative version by constantly brandishing the scars they've gotten for being part of their own camp.

We see it in the stories of people who boast proudly in their bootstrap mentality while withholding compassion from people who are suffering in the ways they have claimed to suffer. We see it when race is a social construct that we shouldn't deign to discuss unless it's time to discuss black-on-black crime. And we see it when black death is worthy of mourning when it happens at the hands of a police officer but not at the hands of a black mother at an abortion clinic.

We see it when that black mother doesn't deserve our compassionate outreach and understanding, but our prejudiced white neighbor does.

We see it all the time. We do it all the time. And all we can do is repent and try anew.

I want the things that I'm learning to equip me to love others better by pointing them to Christ. And I want to do that in word and deed. I want to do that without being a jerk. So I want you to try to take my *do's* and *don'ts* to heart.

And to leave my *well, actually* attitude in the classroom.

Love,

Mama

ELEVEN

You Are a Different Story

Dear Son,

I remember the first time your pappy visited Zambia. He was bubbling over with excitement one evening as I sat in my well-worn chair in his office, reading a book while he worked. We passed so much time together that way, alternately working quietly alongside each other, brainstorming new projects together, or arguing so loudly that your gram came to check on us only to find our good nature intact in spite of the banter.

On this particular evening, though, I wasn't feeling as good-natured as usual. Pappy was going on and on about "the motherland" and how excited he was to visit for the very first time. I sat nervously pretending to listen, but wholly distracted by the question I knew was coming:

"Do you want to come with me?"

Normally, I'd have jumped at the chance to travel with my dad. We've always been close and always had a fantastic time together. He was expecting me to be *thrilled*.

But I was the opposite of thrilled. "No, thanks," I spat out too quickly, shaking my head.

That response launched us into an hour-long verbal battle that I will never forget. I wasn't thrilled at the prospect of going to "the motherland," but terrified. I envisioned warlords and plumbing problems. Where my dad imagined a discovery of some ancestral truth, I recoiled from a very real shame. Why would I want to go to Africa? Didn't all Africans want to wind up here anyway?

You Are Not Shameful

Writing these words is difficult for me now. I'm embarrassed by my ignorance and turned off by my own arrogance. Yet these letters are about telling you the truth.

Son, the truth is I had bought into a stereotype of Africa that made me ashamed to be a descendant of its Western lands.

I could blame Gram and Pappy for this. After all, I was home-schooled. They could have done so much more to teach me about the continent and its varied countries and regions. They could have instilled in me a knowledge of its colorful history as vibrant and captivating to me as the barbarians who conquered the Roman Empire, adopted Byzantine culture, and formed the building blocks of my beloved West.

But they didn't.

And I can't be mad at them for this because as a teacher myself, I've handled years of history curriculum and seen how little the story of Africa appears. Whether I'd gone to public or private school, I still would have been a child of the West and known as much as my peers about Africa and its varied nations.

Which is squat.

It wasn't until their move overseas that my parents began reshaping the way they taught your uncles and aunt about Africa. Now, your uncles and aunt know all of the countries in Africa, their geographical locations, and probably their biggest imports and exports. They know more than the shame I picked up from the books and media, both of which portrayed what our current president might call "shithole countries." Not only that, but they're also learning the hand the West played in shaping Africa's current destiny.

They are learning a more complex narrative than the "West, good; Africa, primitive" narrative I had imbibed.

Blessedly, by the time I actually *did* visit Zambia several years later, I had learned a few things too. Being on Zambian soil taught me even more.

You Know More Than One Story

Over the last year or so, Chimamanda Ngozi Adichie has become one of my favorite authors and thinkers.

It's not that I agree with every single word that comes out of her mouth. It's more of a deep desire to sit across from her and have a conversation. I once found out that the woman doing my hair in a D.C. salon was also Chimamanda's stylist and I literally started shaking. Hands that had touched the hair on that brilliant mind's head were touching my own.

Mama, we made it.

One of my favorite Chimamanda videos is her TED Talk, "The Danger of a Single Story," where she highlights the pitfalls of learning only one perspective, particularly about people. The first time I heard it, my mind instantly went back to that conversation in Pappy's office. I thought about the one narrative of Africa that I had imbibed growing up.

"Show a people as one thing and only one thing over and over again, and that is what they become," Adichie says in her deep, honeyed voice.

When I was ten years old, my dad took us to a summer camp where he was preaching. I met a girl a few years older than me who took me under her wing. She was a beautiful, effervescent blonde with big blue eyes and an adorable pixie haircut that fascinated me. As we walked around the campsite, she stuck her hands in her overalls and said, "I don't know any colored people back home. You're nothing like what I imagined."

I blinked at her, my mouth growing slack for a moment before I recovered and tried to mask my deep offense at being referred to as "colored." I sat there for several minutes while she outlined exactly what she had imagined black people to be like.

I'll let you fill in the blanks, because we've all seen media representation that paints us in a certain light. This young lady was not the only white person I've met who marveled at how "well-spoken" I am or who told me that I'm "not like other black girls."

These people hadn't surveyed black folks. In reality, I was the only black friend most of them had ever had. But they'd arrived at their conclusions about people who looked like me based on a single narrative. The fact that I didn't fit the narrative shocked them.

You'll be the same way, little boy. You'll shock them.

And it won't always be in a good way.

Tribalism is a word you'll hear your daddy and me use often.

What we mean by that will be very clear to you as you grow up playing sports: it's us versus them. Everything you do on that court is supposed to be in service to your team. You even wear the colors that will mark you as a member of the appropriate team, so that in the heat of battle your teammates know who to pass the ball to and who to block.

Adults do the same thing.

Sometimes, we do it politically. Everything we say during election season is in service of either the Republicans or the Democrats, and never the twain shall meet. You're either for my guy or you're against my guy.

Sometimes, we do it theologically. It's been happening since the Corinthian church divided themselves according to followers of Paul and followers of Apollos (1 Cor 1:10-17). We each have our own theological tribe and separate litmus tests to help decide who is for us and who is against us.

Sometimes, we do it ideologically. This one is trickier. These divisions often depend upon buzzwords, and you have to be careful to use the right ones at the right time to signal where you stand on any given issue.

Whichever type of tribalism you encounter, you are sure to make them angry when you start confusing their sorting patterns.

We love to label.

Some labels are helpful. Labeling a theological doctrine saves time in discussion and helps me to make sure we're more or less on the same page. Labeling a person's worldview gives us a grid for understanding what they believe, more or less.

It's always more or less, though. People are complicated and they have a way of seeping outside of their labels. I am a Baptist, but not a fundamentalist. As we get to know people, we realize that one label doesn't completely capture them. We need several.

If we asked our friends to take a label-maker to themselves before church next Sunday, they would be walking around with hundreds of labels sticking on their arms, their legs, and their foreheads. It would take us more than just a cursory glance to read every little thing that described them.

We'd almost be forced to have a conversation with them.

You Cannot Escape Complexity

Pretty soon, you'll learn that while labels can be extremely helpful, they can also quickly become derogatory.

Take the term *SJW* for instance.

Most Christians that I know long to see Christ's justice carried out in society, but far from being an innocuous term the acronym for "social justice warrior" it is often applied as an insult. If my conservative friends refer to an SJW, they mean:

"A person who thinks earthly matters are more important than the gospel."

Or "a person who hates white people and wants them all to submit to a narrative of shame and derision."

Or "a person who doesn't care about abortion as much as police brutality, which is really a myth anyway."

These words become weapons. and their purpose isn't to spur on a productive conversation. It's to shut it down.

We don't want to talk to reach understanding. We want to argue to establish dominance.

People aren't image bearers, but opportunities to force our own viewpoint and stroke our own ideological egos.

We don't want to engage in the complexity of a different story because we truly believe that ours are the only stories that matter.

Here's what we forget: we are members of one body and called to love and encourage each other (Jn 13:35; Rom 12:5; 1 Thess 5:11). Yes, sometimes ideologies need labels. But we need to make sure that we understand each other before we cast out labels. Paul had taken the time to get to know these people, to minister with them, and to spur them on in godliness during an entire epistle. Not just as a passing label thrown in anger.

We may think labels keep our relationships neat and tidy, but often times they only help us escape the messiness of what it means to be truly present in the lives of our brothers and sisters in Christ.

You Can Live a Life Rid of Unfair Labels

If a life rid of this type of tribalism sounds complex to you that's because it is.

You see, it's a lot easier when we allow ourselves to be drawn into the us versus them dogma of present-day dialogues, particularly around race and ethnicity. I've experienced firsthand what happens when I—a black woman—fail to give the secret handshake that lets people on both sides of the aisle know whether I'm an ideological friend or foe.

In one group, if I let certain details slip out, I'm immediately construed as an Uncle Tom, lambasted for trying so hard to serve my white brethren that I've forgotten my roots. My intelligence is called into question, and my black card revoked.

In another, I'm condemned for being a part of the "democratic plantation" (slave analogies are common to both sides, despite what you may hear), and the very nature of my salvation will be up for debate, because I obviously care more about affairs of the world than I do about the mission of Christ Jesus.

Recently, I got drawn into an online debate where I purposefully avoided showing my hand. It only took five comments for the other person in the conversation to start railing against "you all" (see also, "you people") and lumping me in with the viewpoint they despised, which of course, they painted in the least charitable terms possible.

When it comes to tribalism, the rules are simple.

Facts Don't Care About Your Feelings (But They Care About Mine). Each tribe is adept at rattling off its own set of statistics, and each side has its favored statistician. Through these numbers, you are meant to understand everything from black-on-black crime and the systemic injustice of the industrial prison complex to the implicit bias (or lack thereof) of your common police officer. The numbers don't lie, after all. It's our emotions that lie.

But a closer look at anyone's numbers will be enough to tell you that while stats don't have feelings, the people that use them often do. There is always a story behind the data. *Always.* And while it might be tempting to encourage others to pay no attention to the man behind the curtain, it's intellectually dishonest to do so when the numbers sing the song we want to hear.

You Are Full of Unspoken Bias (But I'm Aware of All of Mine). Each tribe is also adept at exposing the hypocrisy of its opponents.

"You are so blinded by your emotions that you can't see what's right in front of you."

"You are so blinded by your prejudice that you don't even realize it."

It's true. We are not clean slates. Each and every one of us have experiences in life that shape the way we view the world. Our understandings are formed by so many outside influences. Added to that is the complexity of trying to read other people's words in light of their own experiences and biases. It's a recipe for disaster, especially when we see ourselves as completely unbiased observers, even as we broad-brush the other team.

Identify Yourself or Be Shot on Sight. The rhetoric of the day allows us to shoot first and ask questions later. If we don't hear the secret knock, we throw a grenade out the clubhouse door and shrug our shoulders at the fallout. If our favorite politician, theologian, or author doesn't identify himself with the right buzzwords, we lop his head off mid-sentence.

James 1:19 tells us that we should be quick to hear and slow to speak, but in the wild west of today's tribalism, we have to speak immediately to let our teammates know we're on their side. And we'd better not be caught listening to the wrong folks too much or we'll be guilty by association.

These rules make for a frightening conversational landscape. It's no wonder we've become so obsessed with tweeting our thoughts to current events right away. We are prideful enough to think we always have all of the facts, arrogant enough to assume we can read those facts without implicit bias, and afraid enough to label ourselves as quickly as possible lest we be cannibalized by members of our own tribe.

You Have a Worthwhile Story

In this particular climate, it can be scary to admit that there might be more than one particular way to approach a certain issue, but I want to raise you to be bold enough to do so.

I want you to embrace different stories.

Here's what I mean: I don't want you to compromise on the Word of God. But I also don't want you to be *un*compromising when it comes to applying the Word of God to a particular circumstance that you haven't observed from every possible angle.

What the Bible says about America's industrial prison complex is clear—if we clearly understand what is going on behind closed doors. The same with immigration, black-on-black crime, and any other statistic that claims to be bandied about without emotional attachment.

But more than understanding the facts behind the numbers, I want you to understand the people whose stories the numbers tell.

One literal way that I want to teach you to do this is by making sure you read diverse stories.

As a twenty-first century Presbyterian child (with two parents who used to be Baptist) who will be educated in a classical school, your role models will have a tendency to take on certain characteristics: white, Protestant, and male.

We have nothing against white Protestant males. We know a great many of them who are wonderful people and who have made incredible contributions to Western thought. We will learn their names unashamedly because there is no shame in their identities.

But there is a likelihood that if we aren't careful to present you with more than a single story, you might end up like teenage Jasmine, convinced that the only contributions worth exploring are the white Western ones and ashamed to be shaped by more than those influences.

So, yes, little boy. You will read the Puritans, because Joseph Alleine's *A Sure Guide to Heaven* fills me with awe at the goodness of God every single time I read it. But you will also read Lemuel Haynes, Charles Octavius Boothe, and Francis Grimke.

My reasoning behind the latter three pastors isn't just because they are black—they are also orthodox and edifying. But their blackness is important not because it changes their status before God, but because I want you to know that God's truth is not limited to white voices. You are not an anomaly. Your godly legacy does not begin and end with Pappy who tends to be the only black man some white Reformed folks know how to quote. Rather, your legacy boasts all kinds of brown men from Athanasius and Michael the Deacon down to your own father.

Christianity is not some white man's religion. It's important to point this out not because there's anything wrong with being a white man any more than there's anything inherently righteous about being a black man. But because there is danger in telling a single story. There is danger in leading you—or just simply allowing you—to believe that Western minds have been the only ones to shape your religious heritage. I want to protect you from idolizing one tribe, because God's truth will be breathed out to each and every one of them before all is said and done.

We already talked about how representation matters in a previous chapter, but it also matters in theology not because skin color dictates truth, but because it illustrates that truth can be breathed out to any skin color. Including your own, which is often incredibly overlooked when it comes to its historical contributions to our faith.

I want you to know about David Livingstone, Lottie Moon, and Jim Elliot. I also want you to know about George Liele (the first Baptist missionary), John Marrant (missionary to the Cherokees), Octavia Victoria Rogers Albert (Christian ethnographer), Mariah Fearing (Bible translator in the Congo), John Chilembwe (nineteenth-century pastor in Malawi), Fanny Jackson Coppin (missionary to South Africa and professor of Latin and Greek), and Dr. Louise Cecilia Fleming (the only black female doctor/missionary in the Congo)—all of whom were brown like you and used mightily by God, as you will be.

I can feel the eyebrows of some of our white brethren raising: what on earth does it matter? But remember that they have not had to walk a mile in your shoes and question whether or not God somehow forgot to include people who look like them into the magnificent story that he is telling. And if he allows me to tarry, you will never have to wonder either.

You Are Free to Tell Your Own Story

My son, I want to teach you all kinds of stories because I want you to understand that the tribes you might be most familiar with do not have the market cornered on truth: God does. And just like Paul, you have got to be able to cut through the tribalistic jockeying for being on the right team to speak a message of unity. We are merely workers in God's field, not mascots to be paraded around in order to prove a point (1 Cor 3:5-9).

You do not owe any tribe your allegiance. You do not owe them any explanation. All that you are called to know is Christ and him crucified (1 Cor 2:2). What I mean is that you are free to withhold your opinion on an issue until you have thoroughly researched it, even if you are pressed for a hot take. You are free to depart from the dogma of a certain tribe if your understanding of God's Word commands it, even when you might be name-called. You are free to maintain neutrality on issues that are not make-or-break gospel moments, even when people want to draw you into a brawl.

You are free, little one. You are free to tell a different story, one rooted in allegiance to Christ, even though it will twist and turn in ways the deeply polarized could have never imagined. You are free to surprise them—all of them—over and over as you question the status quo, carefully examine your own biases, and choose to identify yourself in the ways that God does rather than those of the prevailing cultural narrative.

You are free to learn as many stories as you possibly can and to teach them to others in submission to the one who has been about the business of writing stories since the dawn of time.

As lonely as it may be sometimes, I hope you'll form a community of your own, one that is constantly evolving to become ever more conformed to the image of Christ—not the one-dimensional mascot of a preferred narrative.

Love,

Mama

In Search of Mentorship

Dear Son,

I will never forget that conversation.

I sat across from a mentor talking about what it meant to be black and American. My perspectives were still developing, and she was much more educated than me. She silenced me with quick zingers culled from reading one-sided accounts of American history, and since I had only read those accounts myself, I floundered when pressed. It wasn't until I started reading more that her quick takes resurfaced in my mind and I began to develop long-form answers to each and every one of them.

And yet, we never picked that conversation up again. In fact, our relationship was never quite the same after that day.

When I told a white friend about the conversation, she gaped at me. "Doesn't sound like much of a mentor," she said.

I get it. Not everyone's love language is a heated debate. But that particular debate left me seething because an injustice had been committed. My mentor hadn't wanted to see my point of view. She tried to crush me into submission like a political commentator on a YouTube video that gets circulated around Facebook: "Watch as this seasoned veteran annihilates this idealistic millennial!"

But good mentors are hard to come by, especially as a young black woman. Not because I need a mentor who looks exactly like me, but because I need a mentor who is able to disciple me even when conversations get uncomfortable. And as you know, racial conversations can get uncomfortable.

I have a mentor already. Your pappy.

The other day, I sat down to dinner with someone I was meeting for the first time, and some of their first words were, "So what does your dad think about the way you see social justice issues?"

I smiled genuinely. Usually, I get pretty annoyed when people bring up your pappy within their first few lines of conversation with me. Not because I don't love him—I sincerely do—or because I don't like to talk about my family. But because I get so tired of being known primarily by association with his name.

I worry about you growing up under his shadow because it looms so large over my life that I know it's going to loom large over yours.

Though I know you'll survive it because you will love your pappy as fiercely as I do. That will always outweigh your annoyance with his sycophants and detractors alike.

I hope.

The reason I smiled at this question, though, was because I had just talked to your pappy about the series of letters you're reading now. He said he could not have been prouder of me for writing them. He raised me not to walk in lockstep with his beliefs and ideals, but to be quite comfortable challenging them, which I do. I also know the man behind the ideals and understand that he's more nuanced and complex than a lot of the members of his ideological tribe. I'm proud of him for that, even when I disagree with the friends he chooses.

I know he extends that same love to me.

Your daddy and I are different from your pappy, and you may find yourself different from all three of us. And truly, I hope that we can find a comfortable balance between challenging where we think you're wrong and embracing where we think you're right, as Pappy has done with us.

Sometimes, we aren't brave. Sometimes, we're scared to death. Sometimes, we aren't free of bias. Sometimes, we misstep and show that we're just as cliquish as we claim not to be. But it's a journey, and we're committed to taking it together and dragging you along with us for as long as we can, all the while equipping you with the skills to fly on your own whenever you're ready.

Your flight pattern may not lead you to vote like us, attend the same church, or land on the same side of an ideological issue that we do. But we certainly hope it leads you to prize the Word of God above all else and to use it as your standard for what to believe instead of taking the easy way out and following in our footsteps. Or Pappy's.

We trust that God will give you the grace to do just that, and when the time comes, that he'll give us the grace to let you fly. Whatever your future calling may be, little boy, my one prayer is that it is aligned with biblical priorities and that your heart is most sincerely focused on Jesus in the midst of it. Whether you sprinkle your babies or baptize your teens, become a party man or enjoy the libertarian shock value, have a nine-to-five or become a missionary overseas—to God be the glory.

We hope you're surrounded by mentors. Not just me and Daddy, or Pappy and Gram, but myriad people who are willing to sit with you in the hard places and give you freedom to figure this thing out for God's glory.

I hope I can give you the tools to school them in a historical tête-à-tête too.

But that's secondary.

Love,

Mama

TWELVE

You Are a New Tribe

Dear Son,

When I was a little girl, the one quality Gram always tried to school out of me was my penchant for people pleasing.

You have likely heard the rhetorical question: "If all of your friends were jumping off of a bridge, would you jump off too?"

Back then it wasn't rhetorical for me. I probably would have jumped.

My desire to fit in with my peers and please my authorities was so overwhelming that my first dating relationship imploded when I finally *stopped* trying to please my boyfriend's mother. She felt like she no longer knew me the minute I told her no.

No.

For so much of my life, that two-letter word has been incredibly difficult to form. I used to think it was just a personality trait. Perhaps I was just passive and docile by nature, malleable and mousey.

But my mother knew better. She would shake her head and say, "Your desire to keep friends is going to be the death of you, Jasmine."

It wasn't until I married your daddy that I grew a backbone. Suddenly, incomprehensibly loved by the man I would share the rest of my life with, I was introduced to the girl I'd been hiding from my friends all along. She isn't passive or docile, but principled and a bit high-strung. She is stubborn and headstrong.

She has a fiery temper.

That last one surprised me most of all. Very few people who knew me before I got married would have described me as a girl with a quick temper.

In fact, there were many moments when I was *expected* to be angry and ended up swallowing it back. Like when I wore my hair in its naturally curly state for the first time and a friend told me I looked ridiculous. Or when another friend told me I probably shouldn't try to marry the white boy I had a crush on because our kids would come out looking like freaks. Or after I got married when another friend commented in passing about the "crazy black monkey sex" my new husband and I were probably having.

I should have been angry when my first boyfriend remarked in ways that fetishized my dark skin, full lips, and kinky hair. I should have been livid when he asked me if I'd had a nose job to remove the hereditary flatness he assumed I would want to hide.

I could have been mad when the first boy I ever liked in fourth grade found out about my crush and said—loudly enough for everyone in the class to hear—"Black girls are so ugly. I would never like a girl that looks like Jasmine."

Or before that, when I fell off the monkey bars in elementary school to a chorus of white children singing "nigger monkey, nigger monkey" during my descent.

I don't remember if I was mad, baby. I don't remember if I knew I was *allowed* to be mad. I just remember that I wanted to be liked and accepted so badly that I couldn't show anger. Because I really wanted each and every one of the people who said these things to me to like me. I wanted them to like me more than I wanted them to understand or respect me. I wanted them to like me more than I wanted them to treat me like an image bearer of the most high God.

You Are Allowed to Be Angry

I still struggle to know when it's okay to be angry.

From a Christian perspective, I know that anger is not always sinful. Jesus acted out in righteous anger with the moneychangers defiling his Father's temple (Mt 21:12-13). Paul was rightly angry with the Galatians for subverting the message of the gospel (Gal 2:11-14). Nathan angrily confronted David for victimizing Bathsheba and murdering Uriah immediately after David grew mad at the man in the parable Nathan told to address the king's sin (2 Sam 12:1-14).

Paul tells us how to handle anger in Ephesians 4:26-27: "Be angry and do not sin; do not let the sun go down on your anger, and give no opportunity to the devil."

Be angry, but don't sin in your anger. Do not let it linger and give an opportunity to the devil.

The broader context of this passage is about brotherly love and unity within the body of Christ. In Matthew 18, Christ tells us that the righteous way to deal with an offense is to go to your brother and tell him exactly what he's done (Mt 18:15).

I didn't do that growing up.

In one sense, I didn't know how to do it.

I came from a family full of stiff upper lips. As communicative as we were in our home, our facade toward the outside world had to be pristine. Part of the responsibility we felt to hold it together came from my dad's position, not just as a local pastor, but also as an evangelist who traveled all over the United States and abroad teaching and preaching. To this day, married with two kids of my own, I'm often known as "Voddie's daughter," and it was even more of a shadow over my identity when I lived at home.

Added to those pressures was the burden of being one of the only black families in our area. We were supposed to be exemplary—always. Not just because we were pastor's kids or homeschoolers, but because our brown skin put a target on our backs. It was commonly understood at home that people had certain preconceived notions about black families, and we were supposed to undo each and every one of them.

Son, I realize now that I'm writing it out that this is an incredibly pressured existence. But I don't fault my parents for facilitating it, in part, because I've found myself doing the same thing with you.

When you were eighteen months old and in daycare, you caught the biting bug. I was mortified. There you were, the only black kid in your class, biting my coworkers' children. While the sweet woman who cared for you never once made me feel like a failure of a mom, I was unnerved. What would they think of you—a big-for-your-age black boy—when you started growing and changing in other ways? What would it be like if you were louder than the other kids, more touchy than the other boys, more emotional than people thought you were supposed to be?

What will life be like for you when you're no longer cute and cuddly, and the temper I passed on to you flares in the wrong place at the wrong time? What will they say if your big, tender heart latches on to a white girl?

Of course, the biting phase was developmental. The other children soon began emulating your piranha behavior just as you had given it up in search of a new adventure. But that moment taught me to be merciful to my mom and dad who were trying to teach me how to navigate a world that would see me as different. And they wanted me to be even-keeled instead of perpetually angry, which is admirable.

But I never learned how to be angry at all.

STAND FOR TRUTH

Remember when I said these letters were going to be the musings of a young mom who still doesn't have everything figured out?

Good. Don't forget that.

As I consider who I want to raise in this sharply divided world, I still have so much to learn. But one thing I want to teach you—something that my mom started to teach me with her anti-people-pleasing rants—is that your integrity is more important than fitting in.

The lure of relevancy is strong in any clique, but when it comes with a gag order on truth, it isn't worth it.

If you're anything like me, you'll find yourself dying a slow and painful death to keep your seat at the table if you're not careful. You'll be tempted to let things slide instead of addressing them, all in the name of a conditional acceptance masquerading as love.

Yet it isn't loving to allow your brother to sin against you without letting him know. It isn't loving to build up resentment. It isn't loving to hide your true feelings in order to appear a certain way to your peers.

It isn't really a fruitful relationship if it isn't based on truth. It's actually a bald-faced lie you're telling just to make sure you keep the peace.

I'm not advocating that you scream, "Black power" and throw acid into people's faces when they ask to rub your head. That would fall into the sinful anger category that Paul warns against. What I am advocating is politely looking up from your seat at the table and saying, "Excuse me, but when you said _____, it actually really hurt me." I'm saying that I want to give you the tools to explain exactly why these things hurt and to cultivate in you the patience to do so in love.

And if your friends get mad at you and give up your seat at the cool kids' table, I want you to have the courage to stand up and go sit somewhere else. I want you to know the difference between when it's time to shake the dust off your feet, save your pearls from swine, and form a loving community of believers that challenges one another without the burden of unbiblical guilt over displaying emotions that make the group uncomfortable.

CONTINUE TO BE KIND

Little boy, one of my favorite games to play with you is "Guess What?"

In our version, I'll say, "Hey, Wynnie. Guess what?"

Without fail, your eyes begin sparkling with mischief, and you'll ask me with a grin, "What?"

"I love you!" I'll reply, and before the words are all the way out of my mouth, you'll say, "Love you too, Mama."

We do it about ten times a day, and every single time, you giggle when I shout, "What? Me? You love me? That's awesome!"

The other day on the way home from work, I launched into the game: "Wynnie. Guess what?"

You stared at me petulantly. "No."

"But why not?" I asked in an exaggerated whine.

"Because . . . *I love you!*" you shouted.

And I thought my heart might burst. You are such a sweet, tender-hearted little boy. I hope you never lose that tenderness, even in the face of being misunderstood.

Remember, son: the only one who deserves our complete, unquestioning allegiance is Christ. And even he allows you to ask questions because he is able to bountifully supply the answers. I hope you have the same attitude, one that humbly endeavors to bear with others, at times even up to the point of mistreatment.

Son, I so desire you to keep that tender heart of yours. I so want you to remain kind.

I don't want to teach you these things so that you can thumb your nose at people when you see them falling into traps, but so that you can pull yourself out of them when you fall in yourself.

Because, as sure as you're my son, you will fall in.

And when you do fall, I hope and pray that you are the type of man who will admit that slip and change course. I pray that you are a leader in repentance and that you are the first to display brotherly love.

I want you to know what to do with your anger and I want you to find a community of brothers and sisters who can handle the discomfort of it. And when you do find that community, I hope you realize they won't be perfect, because neither are you. They'll be learning and growing just like you.

You'll know to cast down anchor not when you find the perfect community, but when you find the ones who are striving to be conformed to the image of Christ rather than the patterns of this world (Rom 12:1-2).

Ephesians 4:1-7 is an amazing litmus test:

I therefore, a prisoner for the Lord, urge you to walk in a manner worthy of the calling to which you have been called, with all humility and gentleness, with patience, bearing with one another in love, eager to maintain the unity of the Spirit in the bond of peace. There is one body and one Spirit—just as you were called to the one hope that belongs to your call—one Lord, one faith, one baptism, one God and Father of all, who is over all and through all and in all. But grace was given to each one of us according to the measure of Christ's gift.

Humility and gentleness. Are the people in your community marked by humility and gentleness, even in the face of disagreement? Or are they marked by a constant desire for the warpath? Do they seem more interested in tweeting a zinger than in real-life fellowship and community? Are they about building their own platform and renown? Or are they pursuing the truth, even if it doesn't lead to likes and clicks?

With patience. Do they approach volatile situations with guns blazing? Or are they known to be quick to hear and slow to speak (Jas 1:19)? Do they want you to be able to give a quick, easy answer when it comes to understanding how to relate to you? Or are they willing to do the groundwork of learning?

Bearing with one another in love. Do they seem ready to write people off as soon as someone steps over the tripwire of their least favorite buzzword? Does every conversation feel like a test of your loyalty to their preferred platform? Are they open to dialoguing with you when you say something that strikes them the wrong way? Or are they immediately suspicious of you? How easy is it to lose their respect?

Eager to maintain the unity of the Spirit. What is their unity based on? Is it based on a series of extrabiblical tests? Or is it based on the unity that you have in the truth of the gospel? Paul goes on to remind his readers that there is *one* body, *one* Spirit, *one* Lord, *one* faith, *one* baptism, *one* God and Father of us all. How quick are they to divide over issues that do not touch the heart of this oneness? How quick are they to treat you not as a member, but as *other*?

And how quick are you to fall into these traps yourself? How quick is your current community to overlook when you do? How quick are they to call you on your sin with biblical backing?

How quickly do you find your heart willing to repent?

Forming a new tribe is not easy. It is not for the faint of heart. But as I look out at the ideological landscape you're inheriting, it seems to be the only way forward. And as you form this tribe, realize that it's not all that new at all, but a return to biblical standards for brotherhood that trumps cultural fragmentation every time.

That's what I want for you, little boy.

That's why I'm writing these letters.

May they be a helpful roadmap on the journey forward.

Love,

Mama

Acknowledgments

I have so many people to thank for helping to bring this book to fruition.

This project would not have been possible if Katelyn Beaty hadn't reached out to me. The day we talked about the book, I had just found out I was pregnant with my second born; it is amazing to see both the book and the baby born.

Karen Ellis—"Ma"—gave me the idea to use my "Wynnspiration" to write a book of letters to my son, and gave me the courage to keep writing even when it was hard. Carl Ellis helped me formulate my thoughts in those early stages and get the gears turning. Jackie Hill Perry encouraged me when the book was just a seed.

Don Gates is a stellar agent. Cindy Bunch, my IVP editor, challenged me and stretched me outside of my comfort zone. Keiko Nevers, Jasmine Jones, Portia Collins, Louise Adams, and CJ Leonard were my readers and cheerleaders before anyone else. Barb helped me process so much in these pages. I'm also incredibly grateful to Redeemer Church for the home they've become.

My parents, Voddie and Bridget, poured every ounce of themselves into raising me. It's only now, as a mother myself, that I see just how blessed I am to be their daughter. They gave me room to grow as God's daughter and theirs.

My whole Pickens family—especially my mom-away-from mom, Ophelia, and Florence, Clara, Ida, and Grandmama—loved my husband into the man he is today and watched my little men for me countless times while I wrote.

My own children, Wynn and Langston, are the heartbeat of this book and everything else that I do.

My husband, Phillip, is my champion, my peanut gallery, and my partner in every way. Nothing I do would be possible without his love and support. He is God's sweetest earthly gift to me.

My God has given me too many earthly gifts to name, but these are just a few.

Notes

CHAPTER 1: YOU ARE MINE

12   *In the beginning was the Word:* Part of this section is adapted from Jasmine Holmes, "Nine Months in Mary's Womb: Advent Hope for Mothers," December 5, 2016, desiring God, www.desiringgod.org/articles/nine-months-in-marys -womb.

CHAPTER 5: YOU ARE THE CHURCH

60   *God's promise of a son:* "What Is the Gospel? by Michael Horton," YouTube, February 15, 2011, www.youtube.com /watch?v=caMVMayR690.

65   *When Unitarian minister William Furness:* Joel McDurmon, *The Problem of Slavery in Christian America,* 2nd ed. (Braselton, GA: Devoted Books, 2019), 240.

CHAPTER 10: BE A BRIDGE

102   *One of my very first memories:* Part of this chapter is adapted from Jasmine Holmes, "Be the Change You Want to See on the Internet," April 30, 2018, https://jasminelholmes .com/be-the-change-you-want-to-see-on-the-internet.